Hard Love

Hard Love

A California Memoir

RAY LOPEZ

Foreword by Paula Gill Lopez

RESOURCE *Publications* · Eugene, Oregon

HARD LOVE
A California Memoir

"I Just Want to Get 'Em" was originally published in the Winter 84/85 issue of Joint Endeavor, a literary magazine previously edited and published by inmates at Huntsville State Penetentiary P.O. Box 32, Huntsville, Texas 77340. "Mi Hermanos" was originally published in CQ California State Poetry Quarterly, Summer 1985 Issue Volume XII Number 2. "T.V. Moonlight" was originally published in the Winter 1984 issue of Electrum. "What Does a Poet Look Like" was originally published in the Summer 1983 issue of Electrum THE QUARTERLY POETRY MAGAZINE.

Resource Publications
An Imprint of Wipf and Stock Publishers
199 W. 8th Ave., Suite 3
Eugene, OR 97401

www.wipfandstock.com

PAPERBACK ISBN: 978-1-7252-7994-0
HARDCOVER ISBN: 978-1-7252-7993-3
EBOOK ISBN: 978-1-7252-7995-7

03/31/21

"I do not understand what I do. For what I want to do I do not do, but what I hate I do."

—ROMANS 7:15 (NIV)

"I should have been a pair of ragged claws. Scuttling across the floors of silent seas."

—T.S. ELLIOT,
THE LOVE SONG OF J. ALFRED PRUFROCK

Contents

Foreword by Paula Gill Lopez   ix
Acknowledgments   xiii
1   The Pacific   1
2   Day Labor   4
3   Lost Penis Forestry Camp   10
4   The Wedding   27
5   Gloria Days   34
6   Mexico   37
7   The Drinking Game   40
8   College   45
9   Bezerkely   51
10 Brave Heart   60
11 The Earth Quakes   65
12 Tebben from Heaven   70
13 Baptism   75
14 Take Me Home   77

Foreword

HARD LOVE.
Love is hard. That's not a bad thing. It's how love is meant to be.
Consider these Merriam-Webster definitions of hard:

As an adjective:
not easily penetrated : not easily yielding to pressure
difficult to bear or endure
intense in force, manner, or degree
demanding the exertion of energy: calling for stamina and
endurance
performing or carrying on with great energy, intensity, or
persistence
difficult to comprehend or explain
As an adverb:
with a great deal of effort
so as to be solid or firm

**And sometimes the hardness of love forges diametrically op-
posed tensions pulling at the heart all at once.** Our decision to go
to California was met with joy by Ray's parents and tepid support
by my mother—at first. My mom took me shopping at the Long
Island Arena to buy suitcases for my trip. But as our departure
drew nearer, the thought of her daughter moving 3,000 miles away
gripped her with a knot that closed everything between her gut and
her brain. I am the oldest of six. I came to understand her objection
was to my role of trailblazer—making it easier for the others to follow, to leave her. Love is hard—INTENSE IN FORCE, MANNER
OR DEGREE and sometimes DIFFICULT TO ENDURE.

The day before we left for California, I went out to lunch with friends. When I returned, I found the contents of my bedroom outside on the curb by the mailbox where my mother had put them. The hardness of love can make it DIFFICULT TO COMPREHEND OR EXPLAIN. I was crushed and torn in half wondering if going to California had been the right decision. Looking back, I can see my mom's palpable desperation was fueled at its base to survive. I loved my mother. But I also loved Ray with an all-consuming love NOT EASILY YIELDING TO PRESSURE.

My manager at Beefsteak Charlie's was happy for me when I told him I was leaving to go to California. I'll always remember his parting words—an unlikely mouthpiece of God. He told me in his experience a lot of people go off on life adventures, but they always come back to the same old comfortable, mundane place. He said, "Paula, don't come back. I mean that in the best possible way." And so it was with hard love that DEMANDED THE EXERTION OF ENERGY and CALLED FOR STAMINA AND ENDURANCE that I left as scheduled on September 2, 1980 for San Clemente to begin my life adventure with Ray. I lived in a fog our first year in California—disowned and numb. But in those early days, in small and big ways, we cultivated our relationship with everyday sunshine, fed it with beer, wine, grass, and sunset walks on the beach. And it grew SOLID AND FIRM. We grew up together in Southern California. Hard love was the IMPENETRABLE foundation of our home built by the author and perfecter of love. God is love. ~1John 4:16

Ray regales with this collection of stories in which he recalls how we CARRIED ON WITH GREAT ENERGY, INTENSITY and PERSISTENCE following the road map God set before us. Sometimes, we went down dangerous dark alleys or dead ends where we had to turn around. Rarely did we take the five-lane highway to fast track learning the lessons that brought us closer to Jesus and, as a result, each other.

We've now been married a year shy of four decades. God's grace and mercy incarnate! Somewhere along the way, Jesus whispered the secret to me in two verses. It's the secret to an enduring marriage, but it's also the secret to a life fulfilled.

The only thing that counts is faith expressing itself as love.
~Galatians 5:6
and
Do everything in love. ~1Corinthians 16:14

We aren't promised smooth sailing 24/7. But when we are tossed back and forth like rag dolls on a stormy sea, love is our anchor.

LOVE by its very nature is HARD. But in a good way.
Love never fails. ~1Corinthians 13:8

PAULA GILL LOPEZ

Acknowledgments

"OF THIS I AM confident, that he who began a good work in you will carry it to completion until the day of our Lord and Savior, Christ Jesus." Philippians 1:6

It's the summer of 1982 and Paula and I are driving up the Ortega Highway to see a talent show at Los Pinos. We're in our new Toyota Tercel. We're just out of San Juan Capistrano on a long straightaway before the single lane road starts to climb the mountains. The road descends and elevates creating numerous blind spots ahead. There's an old Chevy pickup truck in front of us doing about 45 miles per hour. We're running late as usual because Paula always gets scattered doing a half dozen things. I pull into the oncoming lane to pass as a tractor-trailer truck roars into view ahead of us. I slow down to pull behind the pickup and he slows down to let me pass! We're side by side; there's no time, no place to go, no discernable shoulder on the side of the road. The 18-wheeler doesn't even try to slow down! As I pull to the shoulder of the road, what little there is of it, our small car tilts at a forty-degree angle, almost tipping over onto the road as the massive truck screams past! At first, we're not sure we're alive. But we start breathing and touching each other and know we survived. I thank Jesus for his continuing faithfulness, mercy, and grace.

I thank my sister, Teresa, the family trailblazer, the one who led the great Lopez California migration. I thank my publisher, Wipf and Stock, for seeing the power of God's love through my stories, and giving this unknown writer an opportunity to share these testimonies with my readers. When I set out to write a memoir I began reading memoirs, searching for writers with similar backgrounds. I discovered James Brown and journeyed through his three books: *The Los Angeles Diaries*, *The River*, and *Apology to a Young Addict*. His writing drew me deep into the story of his survival and victories. His ironic use of present tense narrative brought immediacy to his memories, bringing his readers closer to his thoughts and feelings. I hope I have come close to what he has accomplished in this book and my third memoir, *Hard Faith*. I thank my brother Steve for helping to sharpen my memories of our time together on the West Coast. I thank Paula for being my Proverbs 31 wife, my best friend, my confidant, my counselor, my love. This is our California story.

1

The Pacific

YES AS WE STEP out into the blazing bright California sun of the city of angels I become planted through the concrete deeply rooted in ancestral soil I throw my head back spread my arms wide and breathe in deeply the Holy Spirit sun yes a new son a second life a small moment forever and so it goes yes

The day after my 21st birthday, with my arm around Paula, I feel solid ground beneath my feet, below the concrete. After living our lives on Long Island, we are off on our great exploration of the heart. It seems that whenever we were together before leaving, we heard *Sailing*, by Christopher Cross, on the radio and felt a deeper connection, a stirring in our hearts, an affirmation of our destined journey . . . and we hear it again on the radio playing over the speakers outside the terminal at LAX—"*Sailing takes me away to where I've always heard it could be/Just a dream and the wind to carry me/And soon I will be free.*" It's one of our songs. I sang it in a rowboat during our courtship on Wells Lake in Smithtown. We are an unorthodox couple. She did the rowing. I did the singing. We fit together perfectly like the first pieces of a new puzzle at the right angle. Her straight blonde hair cascades just past her lean, muscled upper back, shining a new bleached blonde brilliance. We sit on our suitcases and wait and watch people—happy, hugging California sun people, with their tanned skin, muscular surfing bodies in shorts and sandals, bright blue and hazel eyes; and their deep brown skin, longed baked through the centuries, with many tattoos, short, dark black hair, dark brown eyes, wearing khakis and white, sleeveless tee shirts; and their pale skin, Asian eyes, restrained embraces; and their bodies, multiple shades of black glistening arms and legs, afros, and cornrows.

In some ways we are both escaping from New York, from what we've known, and some of those who have known us in that light and the shadows. We know nothing but the love we feel and believe will be enough.

Teresa and her boyfriend, Brad, come walking up, rubbing sleep from their eyes, apologizing for being late; not Sonny and Cher, more like Shady and Cher. Brad, long and lanky with light brown hair, has a thin mustache and goatee, and a slow Southern drawl. He's originally from Florida and calls Teresa "Darlin." With the sun setting soon, we decide to smoke some weed on the way to our new home but to first go to the beach off the San Clemente Pier to see our first Pacific sunset. Taking I-405 South to I-5 South, we have plenty of time to party, packed into long lines of people driving home after long days of work as the rays of the sun bounce off hoods and windshields. I notice an immediate difference compared to driving back east on the Long Island Expressway. We don't hear any angry horns honking, just the sounds of motors running, and music, a blend of Spanish Folk and Classic Rock.

By the time we get to the Pier, the sun is halfway gone below the sea-green horizon, painting a brilliant portrait of colors with brushes of clouds—pink, orange, lavender, red—beautifully diffracted by the polluted sky. There are only a few surfers riding the gentle waves. The second we park, Paula jumps out of the van and sprints toward the water, her blue-and-white-striped sundress flapping in the breeze. She runs straight toward the golden path glistening along the surface, calling only to her. She walks in and as she heads out toward the edge of her world, with one hand in each side pocket, she lifts the bottom of her dress as each wave splashes through her and crashes to shore. We sit on the sand and light another joint. Eventually she emerges and slowly strides back to shore. She has great posture but there's now something majestic in her gait, something new in her eyes. Beads of water sparkle from her hair and drip down her face, so at first I don't see that she's crying. We embrace and the trembling floodgates open, then slowly subside into deep breaths. She suddenly realizes that her wallet is gone with the waves. It slipped from her pocket, with all her IDs, as she raised her arms in worship while trying to keep her dress dry. And she starts laughing in the joy of Christ, who baptized her in the Pacific and gave her a new identity and a new life.

"You were taught, with regard to your former way of life, to put off your old self, which is being corrupted by its deceitful desires: to be made new in the attitude of your minds; and to put on the new self, created to be like God in true righteousness and holiness." Ephesians 4:22–24 (NIV)

2

Day Labor

SAN CLEMENTE IS A little beach town about halfway between San Diego and L.A. in Orange County, the Republican epicenter of the state. It is mostly populated by White middle-to-upper-middle-class native Californians and out-of-staters from the Midwest and back East. Although there is a heavy presence of Chicano gang life in Orange County—the largest being F Troop, based in Santa Ana—the homeboys have not yet settled into our new haven. The people are "laid back" and live in rhythm with the daily ebb and flow of the tide. The professionals, lawyers, doctors, corporate types, all hit the waves before and after work, and the kids model their parents. Camp Pendleton, the Marine Base, is only ten miles south down the freeway. A lot of Jarheads rent near the beach, which is a popular place for recruits to party.

Our new home is just east of the freeway in the low hills, and we arrive to find a change of plans. Teresa's and Brad's roommates, Rick and his stripper girlfriend, Suzy, have not yet moved out, and Paula and I find ourselves sleeping on a mattress at the foot of the waterbed in Teresa's and Brad's room. We are starting off on the floor. No place to go but up. Everything is new and there is so much we don't know. We have yet to make love.

Rick has bad skin and long, oily red hair. He's average height and weighs about a buck-and-a-half with that sunken-skin look from sucking the life out of his veins through a needle. He manages the strip club where Suzy dances. Rick has a Great Dane named Brutus, and Teresa reports that she walked by their bedroom one night and saw a picture of hell through a slight opening in the door—bestiality. They move out after a couple of weeks, and we all move out a week or so later. I don't know how they ended up living in this house together, but Rick is a bad actor apparently capable of attempted murder.

Driving to the work one morning, Teresa has to pull off the freeway because her van starts shaking up a storm once she reaches 65 MPH. The lug bolts had been loosened. Rick was the suspect as he was seen by Frog mulling about the driveway early that morning with a cup of Joe in his hand and a cigarette hanging from his mouth. Frog, a bricklayer/mason, works for Brad and waits in the driveway each day before they head out. Problems persist with Rick, primarily over ownership of certain household items. He insists that the refrigerator is his and comes to claim it while we're at work. Teresa can hold her own and is able to dissuade him for the moment but not before he makes threats. No one threatens my sister without feeling my wrath—a long-established doctrine. That night I call Rick at the strip club and tell him to stay there so I can come and rip the eyes out of his head. He suddenly sees the light through the eyes he wishes to keep and says there's no need for violence. I agree upon the condition that we never hear from him again. We never hear from him again. I'm still angry much of the time, which makes loving me hard.

During the next couple of months, we move two more times with Teresa and Brad before arriving at our own one-bedroom apartment at 1002 Buena Vista. Situated across the street from the condos on the bluff overlooking the beach, we have our tiny ocean view between them. The stairs leading down to 204, a local surf spot, are seconds from our front door.

After a short stint as a Betty Crocker sample hostess at the local supermarket, Paula starts waitressing at a Howard Johnson's. I'm working as the laborer of a three-man crew. Brad's father has a contractor's license and is able to finesse enough masonry jobs to keep the one-truck outfit going. It's hard to know how old Frog is because he has that weathered, worn out, heavy-living look. He stands about five-feet-something, weighs about 125 lbs. and has thick, shoulder-length blond hair and a Fu Manchu mustache. His skin tone is reddish-brown. They call him Frog because he sort of croaks when he speaks, a result of a lifetime of smoking all kinds of stuff. And he talks a lot, so he sounds like a croaking frog that follows you around. He's married to a pretty young brunette named Peaches. She's 19 years old, about a half-a-foot taller than Frog and a full-bodied woman, probably outweighing him by 50 lbs. They are a startling couple and just had a baby girl named Regan, after Linda Blair's character in *The Exorcist*.

Our days on the crew start with a couple of joints, then picking up supplies: some egg sandwiches for breakfast with black coffee and a 12-pack of Budweiser and ice for the cooler. We meet the cement truck at the site, and I start hauling cement in a wheelbarrow and lugging bricks to stack them near the wall. And so it goes, back and forth, cement and bricks, break for lunch, another joint, deli sandwiches and beer, and back and forth, cement and bricks, until we run out of sun and leave, and tomorrow and tomorrow and tomorrow. I'm not feeling the love for Brad because I'm not seeing, not feeling his love for my sister. He's a heroin addict abstaining for a time and getting by on weed and beer; and he's a dog, howling at every good-looking woman we see, like I won't care because he thinks I'm like him. On one occasion he even makes a comment about Paula's ass. After a couple of days of this shit, I can't sit in the front of the truck anymore, so I ride in the back with the supplies and tools. I hear them joking on the way home one day that we're like every other crew with a Mexican in the back of the truck. Brad nicknames me "Lips" because I have big lips and he thinks he's funny. And this takes me back to my dark childhood—my dark skin, the taunts of nigger and spic—and anger boils in my gut.

One weekend, we all take off for a campground in the Cleveland National Forest where there's a cliff with a small waterfall. We're in two vans; Teresa, Brad, Peaches, and Regan in one, and Paula and I are driving with Frog. This is a Chaparral Forest rich with Manzanita plants with blood-red branches, topped by tall pines and sagebrush rolling across the valley floor. It's full of mountain lions, bobcats, Mexican red rattlers, copperheads, tarantulas, and scorpions. It's an

DAY LABOR

exciting and sometimes dangerous place. We smoke a lot of weed and drink beer and some Mescal tequila with the mythical worm in the bottle. We hike out a mile or so to the waterfall. There's a small pool at the bottom with a circumference of about 25 feet. It's deep enough in the middle, but there's a ledge of rock about five feet around the edges, which is only a few feet in depth. There's a spot about 20 feet up the rock where you can jump from, or you can go from the top, a 40-foot drop. The challenge is to launch yourself far enough toward the middle of the pool to avoid smashing onto the shallow sides. It is relatively easy from 20 feet, but 40 feet is crazy enough sober, and psychotic if you're drunk and stoned. Everyone else jumps from 20. I jump from 40. A dead-center landing in the ice-cold water sobers me up slightly, but I'm buzzing with an adrenaline rush and make another successful jump, another example of God's mercy in spite of my need for crazy. That night we finish the tequila, and I swallow the worm hoping for a psychedelic experience. It's just a plain old worm . . . and I'm just plain old wasted.

The next morning we pack up to leave. You pay for the site on the way out. Teresa and Brad, Peaches and Regan are already on the road. We have no money and find out that Frog also has no money and no intention to pay as he drives through the gate, smashing it in two and sideswiping the park ranger who is waving at us to stop. And we're off, racing down this mountain road with this crazy, hung over beach bum turned desperado. We have no idea where we are or where we're going.

In no time a highway patrol unit is behind us with lights flashing and sirens wailing. Fortunately, Frog doesn't think it wise to engage law enforcement in a high-speed chase along a desert highway. They impound the van and transport us to the station. Paula and I are freaking out. We're in California just three weeks and now sitting in a highway patrol station in we don't know where. I'm off probation for like a month and we're with this drunken fool asshole, who has a little man's complex and doesn't give a shit. We spend the entire day at the station before the cops determine we were innocent passengers and let us go.

We have no money and no way to contact my sister, so we start walking along State Route 70-something, trying to hitch a ride.

We're successful (again I'm in the back of a truck) and get dropped off at a real redneck cowboy bar. We walk in. The talking stops; the jukebox keeps playing country music. The sun set long ago, and the bar is packed with the after-dinner regulars: cowboys wearing their cowboy hats and boots, buying drinks for their cowgirls, wearing their cowgirl hats and boots. I'm wearing a muscle shirt and shorts, and Paula is in her white bikini top and blue jean short shorts. The cowboys stop shooting pool and throwing darts, the country music keeps playing, and all eyes are on us. What a sight. I don't know, but I imagine they're thinking I'm a Mexican pimp working my green-eyed blonde who I kidnapped in Ensenada. We just stand there, unsure what to do when Teresa and Brad walk in, and we make a fast exit, get in the van, and take off. They'd been looking for us all day. They finally backtracked to the campsite and found out what happened. As a last resort, they went to the closest highway patrol station and got the news. This was their last stop before heading home. Mercy, mercy, mercy.

Jumping from the top of the waterfall

Safe and unsound

"Who is a God like you, who pardons sin and forgives the transgressions of the remnant of his inheritance. You do not stay angry forever but delight to show mercy." Micah 7:18 (NIV)

3

Lost Penis Forestry Camp

AT REGAN'S CHRISTENING I meet Peaches' brother, Jim. At the party, we talk, and he tells me that he works as a group night counselor at Los Pinos Forestry Camp, a county-run juvenile detention facility in the Ortega Mountains, near Riverside County. He tells me they are looking to hire a new deputy night counselor and I should apply. This is a Godsend, as I am dying each day I work off the back of the truck. I don't have any college, but I do have six months' experience as a group counselor at Saint Mary's of the Angels in Syosset and a month at a nearby group home.

The Ortega Highway, State Route 74, is a winding snake of a road. It climbs up the mountains from just above sea level in San Juan Capistrano to an altitude of over 4000 feet before descending into Lake Elsinore, where they claim their own Lock Ness-type monster. Los Pinos sits at the summit. San Juan is a bird sanctuary. Every year around the Day of San Juan, October 23, the famous cliff swallows swirl into the sky to return to their wintering grounds in Argentina, 6000 miles south. And they faithfully return every spring in mid-March, a celebration of the cycles of life.

The Ortega Highway, also known as "The Highway of Death," is infamous in claiming more deaths per mile than any route in the state. It runs 30 miles to Los Pinos and another 15 down to the lake. Once you hit the hills, it winds and turns continuously, at times along the edge of 400-foot drops into the rocks and San Juan Creek running below. At one point, motorcycle riders actually painted a red starting line in San Juan and a finish line at Lookout Point above the lake. A lot of riders were wiped out by this race. There are truckers, campers, and commuters, all driving on "The Highway of Death," and one day we almost lose our lives.

It's the summer of 1982 and Paula and I are driving up the Ortega to see a talent show at Los Pinos. We're in our new Toyota Tercel. We're just out of San Juan Capistrano on a long straight-away before the single lane road starts to climb the mountains. The road descends and elevates, creating numerous blind spots ahead. There's an old Chevy pickup in front of us doing about 45 MPH. We're running late as usual because Paula always gets scattered doing a half dozen things. So I pull into the oncoming lane to pass just as a tractor-trailer truck roars into view about 100 yards ahead of us. I immediately take my foot off the brake to slow down and pull in behind the truck but he slows down to let me pass! We're side by side; there's no time, no place to go, no discernable shoulder on the side of the road. The 18-wheeler doesn't even try to slow down! As I pull to the shoulder, what little there is of it, our small car tilts at a 40-degree angle, almost tipping over onto the road as the massive truck screams past! At first, we're not sure we're alive. But we start breathing again, touch each other, and know we survived.

The mountains also provide a good place to dump a body, sort of a west coast Staten Island. A murderer could easily pull off at one of the many turnouts along the cliffs and just toss a body over the edge, with nary a soul around for miles in any direction. Sometimes the vultures help the troopers find the body.

Toward the beginning of November, I get an employment application from Jim, fill it out, mail it in, and receive a letter in response inviting me to come up for an interview. I find myself sitting in Von Roley's office. He's the camp director, an older man in his late 60s, with dark, deep wrinkles in his forehead and cheeks. He has a hawkish nose, thick eyebrows, and a dark, brooding stare. And he's a little bent over. The assistant director, Carlos Rosas, is a Chicano in his mid-40s, with round facial features, dark black hair, and brown eyes. And he's a little overweight.

I'm doing well in the interview, talking about my experience (all seven months of it) and my excitement about working with gang members to help them turn their lives around. I figure the more I talk, the fewer questions they'll ask; then Mr. Roley asks, "Have you ever been arrested or convicted of any criminal offense?" My first instinct is to lie—the thought of sin, which always presents itself before the act. I stop, think deeper, and speak the truth. I tell the story, explaining the unique set of circumstances behind what you see on my rap sheet, just in case they were to get a copy of it. Of course I don't tell them about all the drugs I've done and the time I spent in a psychiatric hospital. My story is the classic all-American rebel, too much youthful drinking and fighting; I learned a great lesson about consequences and responsibility, and I am ready to share my insights with the lost and wandering youth. I am very wise at the age of 21. I end the interview with, "Being on probation was an eye-opening experience for me, and it's why I have chosen to work in the field. I received an early release from supervision on September 6, a few days after I moved to California with the court's permission. Here's my release certificate; you can call Mr. Roselloe and he will be happy to discuss our time together." This is the first of many similar statements to come during interviews that lay ahead, explaining my criminal history and leaving the interviewer thoroughly impressed by the insights I gained into myself and others on my journey through the system.

So thanks to Carlos Rosas, less than two months after receiving an early termination from probation, I am hired by the Orange County Probation Department as an on-call, group night counselor. I come to find it wasn't my magnificent presentation during the interview, during which Von Roley barely stayed awake. In his day, Carlos Rosas was a hellraiser back in the Barrio in San Bernardino, and I remind him of himself.

Los Pinos used to be a Job Corp facility and is owned by the U.S. Department of Forestry and Agriculture. Orange County rents the complex from the federal government for one dollar a year in exchange for thirty percent of the work force being devoted to cutting fire breaks in the mountains, clearing trails, and maintaining several campgrounds within the Cleveland National Forest. It houses approximately 100 juveniles between the ages of 13 and 18. Seventy-five percent are Chicano gangbangers from Santa Ana, Anaheim, Orange, Buena Park, Brea, and Fountain Valley. F Troop, based primarily in Santa Ana, is one of the oldest, largest, most organized gangs in the county. These kids have been sentenced by the court to anywhere from 6-to-18 months for crimes such as armed robbery, burglary, assault with a deadly weapon, auto theft, larceny, and sexual assault. I'm only a couple of years older than some of these guys. There are six dorms holding up to 16 wards, a large cafeteria, a gym, the front office, and dorms for the staff. Los Pinos sits in a small valley shadowed by hiking trails to the north. There is also a trailer park next to the camp where Carlos Rosas and some of the supervisors live. Deputy probation counselors work three-day shifts, two 16-hour days and eight hours on the third day. We have no transportation when I first start, so I hitch up the mountain to get there by 10:30 p.m. to cover my shift. As long as I get on the road by 6:00, I usually make it on time. There are some small village communities in the mountains, including a nudist colony along the same road that leads to the camp. They must've been shy because I never saw any naked people. People commute to the beach cities from some of these places, some from Lake Elsinore, and there are always truckers hauling stuff back and forth. Some folks know about Los Pinos and drive me up the two-mile road off the highway that takes you to the camp and Blue Jay Campground further up. The road is steep and rises about 1500 feet. Sometimes I have to hike it at night.

The graveyard shift is tough. The dorms are open with two sets of bunk beds in each room. Escapes are rare because most of these guys haven't traveled five miles from their barrios, and now they're in the mountains in the middle of nowhere. But I have to stay alert because shit happens. Less than two weeks into the job, I learn about the Santa Anas, strong downslope winds that blow through the mountain passes in Southern California, easily exceeding 40 MPH. They are warm and dry and can severely exacerbate brush or forest fires, especially during a drought. Southern California had been in a severe drought since the late '70s, and fires have already started in the fall.

I make it up the mountain by 9:30 that night. I'm relaxing in the office before heading to the dorm when I hear sirens going off. I step out and see an orange glow in the southern sky. Counselors are marching their groups to assemble in front of the flagpole at the head of the office parking lot. We assemble there every morning before breakfast for count, so the group comes together quickly. There are 96 kids, 12 counselors and three supervisors, but only two 16-passenger vans, a few trucks, and a tiny fleet of personal vehicles are available. We pack the boys into the vehicles like sardines, and I'm assigned to ride in the back of—what else?—a truck to provide supervision.

It's 30 miles down the Ortega to I-5, then 20 miles north to the Juvenile Hall in Santa Ana. We're scared on the truck, leaning against the wood sides, praying they hold up against the weight of our bodies, swaying side-to-side, as the driver leans into the curves and turns as we wind down the highway. And we watch the long snake of fire, slithering across the southern mountain ridges for miles; its frightening power is beautiful. We have miles to go before we sleep that night.

After a couple of months, I'm hired as a full-time counselor and begin my seven years on the mountain. I start off with a Saturday through Monday shift but eventually get a Monday through Wednesday spot. This schedule opens up the rest of the week for working out with Paula at the San Clemente Health Club and taking courses at Saddleback Community College in Mission Viejo, a few exits north up the freeway. Paula and I purchase a black Ford Econoline van, a commercial model with no windows on the sides. It has a bad starter but is a standard, so a running pop-the-clutch start is doable. This requires strategic parking on the downward side of a hill and sometimes offers me great training opportunities pushing the van fast enough to start it. It's a simple process of pressing down on the clutch, putting the van in first gear and releasing it once you gain enough speed, which jump starts the engine. One night while picking me up at the camp, Paula parks in the visitors' lot instead of the road leading to the front gate which has enough downgrade to get us going. It takes a herculean effort on my part, pushing the van across the lot several times before it starts. I finish a six-pack by the time we get down the mountain and see the lights of San Juan, which always bring me joy.

Half the boys attend school in the morning, and the other half work on either the forestry, painting, landscaping, or maintenance crews. The groups switch during the afternoons. I end up with the painting crew, part-time, run by Jesse Gomez, who was a commercial painter for twenty years before making a radical career change. I learn enough to be a painter and so do a lot of the boys. Being on the forestry crew is a cool job. We hike out on the trails and use Mattocks and McLeods (trail clearing tools) to cut back the fire breaks. I learn not to step over a log onto the shady side where you might stir a resting rattler. The snakes are necessary to keep the rodent population down, so we keep a steel shovel in the sun for when we cross one. They're easy to spot because they rattle to let you know they're there. You just point the head of the shovel near the snake and it will strike in reaction to the heat, knocking itself semi-conscious. Then you just scoop it up and toss it away.

There's an auto shop across from the cafeteria and a number of storage sheds in the same area, which provide plenty of cool spots for those Mexican Red rattlers to rest. Pat, the school secretary, is a manly woman. She's in her mid-40s, has blonde hair and played softball in college. Her weekends are spent hunting rattlers, skinning them to make belts and hatbands to sell, and cooking and eating the meat. She tells me that if I ever come across a rattler, she'll catch it and make me a belt or a hatband. One morning I'm assigned to supervise the maintenance crew, which this day is a one-man operation because the other guy's out sick. We finish up with the trash and general cleaning duties early and are just hanging around. I cherish these opportunities for some one-on-one time with a kid to do *counseling*. I have the keys to all the buildings, and we walk up to this shed, which I have never explored.

I unlock it, and the second we swing the wooden doors outward, we're confronted with a fat Mexican Red right behind the door a few inches away. The snake is very disturbed by our intrusion, rattling furiously as it fortunately slithers toward the back of the shed. The structure is about 12-feet deep, six-feet wide, and there are two sets of crossbeams holding two catamarans—sailboats with two parallel sections connected by a strong nylon fabric and a frame for the sail post in the center. We don't have a sailing program, so I have no idea why these boats are even there. The snake is now trapped in the back of the shed and really pissed off. I send my charge off to get Ms. Thomas.

Pat comes running up with the kid right behind her. She's carrying her "snake stick," which is a 5½-foot broomstick handle with a rope noose attached at the end through a drilled hole. She quickly assesses the situation and immediately comes up with her strategy. The four crossbeams are set four feet back from the door and rear wall. Our friend is in the back corner rattling away. Pat will climb onto the top boat and crawl toward the back, where she will lower her snake stick and catch the reptile. This requires that we hold each end of the two sections of the boat, as Pat's bodyweight could otherwise cause it to tip, dropping her onto her prize . . . which would be really bad. Before we can agree (or protest), she is up on the boat and slowly moving her way back on her hands and knees. The snake sounds angrier, rattling faster and louder. Pat keeps moving. She slowly reaches down, slips the noose around the snake's neck and starts lifting it off the floor, but it wrestles free before she can tighten the noose. It falls to the floor about halfway from the door and starts slithering in our direction!

In the split second that I have to decide whether or not to release the boat to avoid getting bit, Pat reaches down with her snake stick, slips the noose around its head, tightens it and lifts the snake off the floor, only inches from my feet. She's got it secured. She crawls forward holding the snake out in front and carefully extracts herself from the shed, proudly displaying her catch. It's about 3½ feet long, and fat, easily two inches across in diameter. Pat points out that there are twelve rings around the rattle, which means this snake is an old-timer as a new ring forms each time it sheds its skin. We stand in awe, speechless. Pat grabs the snake just under its head, draws her Schrade Buck knife and smoothly cuts off the head, which falls to the pavement with a soft thud.

We're still without words, mouths agape, inviting gnats. "Watch this!" she says and places the blade inside the snake's mouth, which, disembodied, bites down hard on the blade with two protruding fangs, shooting its milky venom across the steel. She explains that the snake's brain and nervous system is still active for a time and will react to heat and strike even when the head is decapitated. Pat places the head in a small burlap sack, grabs the body and says, "Let's have an early lunch," as she heads for the kitchen.

She peels the skin, just like pulling the skin off a cooked sausage, and hands the snake to Armon, the head cook. This is not his first snake. He slices the meat off into fillets, breads them in buttered batter, then deep-frys the meat until it's golden brown and crispy. Of course it tastes like chicken. I buy a big, brown cowboy hat for the hatband Pat makes for me. I don't wear it much, but the skin stays with me as an office decoration during my long career and provides many opportunities to tell this story.

The boys of Los Pinos, or Lost Penis, as we call it, are mostly from the same place. They're from different barrios but the same culture. They are second- or third-generation "Chicanos," Mexican-Americans in the 1980s. They are separated by different cities and sometimes by just a couple of blocks. These lines were established 50 years ago. The social clubs or car clubs their fathers joined for community and protection have evolved into violent, territorial groups that battle it out to claim the fruits of a meager existence financed by selling drugs and stealing from each other. Their grandparents—and sometimes their parents—are poor field workers. They are from the same provinces in Mexico, eat the same food, listen to the same music and worship the same Virgin Mary; but they are separated by a hatred that has been slow cooking for decades. In hating each other they hate themselves, but they don't see it that way.

I love the job. Since I'm obviously from New York and talk like a New Yawkah, the boys think I'm Puerto Rican. Some of them make progress, learn a trade and earn their diploma or GED, but they go back to the same streets and return to us again and again. I have one young man on my caseload I watch grow from 13 to 18. Joe and I have a love/hate relationship. I love him and sometimes he hates me. You have four boys on your caseload. You are to pour your time into mentoring, counseling, and guiding them in life, but you can't connect with everyone. You do what you can. I spend most of my time with the 16 boys in my dorm.

A couple of the finer counselors are into Carl Rogers' book, *On Becoming a Person*. These men have been on the mountain for a while, and I see how effective they are and the respect they receive in return. So I develop some skills running groups like one the boys call *The Hot Seat*. I think Rogers refers to it as *The Listening Seat*. It's mostly an exercise to enhance honesty and open communication within the group. The listener sits in a chair in the middle of a circle. Then each resident is to say something they appreciate or don't appreciate about the listener, who can only say "thank you" or "got it" until everyone has a turn. Thereafter, I attempt to facilitate an open discussion of what was shared. It's hard. The boys are angry, guarded, and full of rage and shame. They've seen a lot and felt a lot of pain: drug-addicted, alcoholic parents, incarcerated parents, good parents that can't keep them from the streets, or no parents, just grandma or nobody, violence in the house, on the streets, shootings, stabbings, beatings, and death. And they grow older and turn into angry, violent young men who don't expect to live long.

Sometimes I have to work the graveyard shift if the night counselor doesn't show, and sometimes I hear their fear, their pain, their anger, their love, their hearts; I am moved to see some light in each moment. I am the Watchman each night . . . and tomorrow and tomorrow and tomorrow.

WATCHMAN
"Watchman, what is left of the night?"
The Watchman replies,
"Morning is coming, but also the night.
If you would ask, then ask;
and come back yet again." Isaiah 21:11

Waking hours
hiding
                        behind their masks.

Put on
like armor.

Lights out at 9:30
but there's no escape
in the night.

LOST PENIS FORESTRY CAMP

The dream wars begin.

Listen to them
wrestling with the enemy
talking to God
Pagas con tu meurte
el pendejo.

And it gets loud
when they start
screaming like
Go ahead shoot me vato! Shoot!
I'll kill you ese!
Mamá lo siento.

Throbbing restlessness,
call it sleep
Fightin' them dream wars
Watchman, what is left of the mind?

Oscar is on my caseload. He's from Santa Ana, a member of
F Troop and Junior F Troop before that. He's 10 when he starts as
a lookout for police or rival gangs coming down the block. At age
12, he works as a runner of product, mostly heroin and some weed,
going back and forth between the stash and seller, seller and buyer.
At 14, he starts selling PCP, or "Wack." They soak a joint in liquid
PCP and sell you a "Sherm." Oscar never met his father, and his
mother is in Tijuana.

He is being raised by his abuela, along with his three younger
siblings. She is on state assistance and sells tamales on the street.
Oscar's probation officer tells me a story about an attempted home
visit. She gets out of her car and starts for the house when she is ap-
proached by a young Chicano man wearing his beige khakis, belted
high at the waist, his Pendleton shirt—the uniform for vatos—and
the bandana cutting across his eyebrows. When he asks her what
she needs, she displays her badge and the young man tells her, "That
doesn't get you any discounts around here."

Oscar is short, about 5½ feet tall and has dark-brown skin and
sort of a flat, pudgy face. He knows how to get by. He has a soft,

gravelly voice, and he's smart and artistic. He draws sketches, and he's a graffiti artist. Everybody likes Oscar. He's got respect. He only sells drugs for a short time before he's seen by the gang for his true calling. Oscar is a shooter. He is one of the troopers who protects the drug spots, the block, the barrio. He's been in several shootings, and he's only 15 when I meet him. We are tight and spend a lot of time talking after lights out. He tells me about the drive-by shootings and the homeboys he has lost. He has their names tattooed on his body. He is calm—steely—when he tells me his stories. Sometimes he stares off beyond the four walls. He's killed people but doesn't like to talk about it. He talks about his love for his abuela, his hermanos and hermana, his homies, and I want to know what he thinks and feels when in battle and why. Over time he is able to explain, and I come to understand his life and reasoning.

I Just Want to Get 'Em

I just want to get 'em, blow 'em away! With my .45
they'll hear what I say.

I don't care.		You
Let em' die.	.sold	got
Because man.	is	to
That's why!!!	Death	do
I just want to get	,man	it.
'em, Don't you see?	first	It's
If I don't get them	it Sell. cold not	
They'll get me!!!		

Hector is also on my caseload. He's big for 16, standing six-foot-something and weighing about 200 pounds. He's jacked from lifting weights and is a good athlete. He can ball on the court. He's menacing. I don't know much about his story. He's guarded and feared. I know from his file that Hector is a full-blown criminal who doesn't discriminate. He'll stick up a drug spot as well as rob an old lady. In Matthew 6: 22, 23 God says, "The eye is the lamp of the body. If your eyes are healthy, your whole body will be full of light. But if your eyes are unhealthy, your whole body will be full of darkness. If then the light within you is darkness, how great is that darkness!" If 90% of communication is nonverbal, I'd say it's mostly in the eyes. Hector's eyes are dark, like black holes. If I dare look deep enough, I imagine that I can't see my reflection, that I can't see any light. But there *has* to be some light. Hector is human. He has a family. He's a heroin addict, which is his sole motivation. He is still alive and can still love but it's . . .

LOVE TO DEATH
She makes love to your blood.
But when it's over,
there's no resolution,
only mad desire.

You were kickin' it
with your homeboys and
like a shot in the night
she came, Ms. Cargá.
You were a virgin
but you couldn't back down.
Everybody was makin' it with her
and getting' off!

It went in so easy
and man the feelin!
Noddin' off
you floated off the floor forever.
But when you came down
the memory was like breathin'.
You heard her voice,
felt her heart,
faint at first,
then louder and louder and louder!
You had to have her
take you in,
again, and again, and again . . .
Nothing else mattered.

Poor infected child.
You knew nothing.

She caught you in her web,
this black widow.
Only her kind
takes years to devour her lover.
She bites off and eats a small piece
of your body
and each time she leaves
you pray for her return.

There are very few escape attempts from Los Pinos because there are many dangers in the mountains. We receive Poisonous Plants and Critter Training every year. In addition to rattlers there are copperheads, a highly venomous species, which can often be mistaken for a coral snake. The thing to remember regarding the telltale color combinations on the skin is: *"Black and yellow, friendly fellow; black and red, you are dead."* The tarantulas are the size of your hand but not poisonous. They are bird spiders with a sort of sideways beak for a mouth, and if you scared one it could bite you and make you bleed. There are magic mushrooms to be found, but mostly poisonous mushrooms that took out a number of young lads on the forestry crew looking for a natural high. You are warned not to walk around barefoot lest you step on a scorpion, which will make you very sick. A bite from a black widow or brown recluse spider could result in a trip to the hospital to lance and drain the infectious puss. And there are mountain lions. In one case of attack, a lion came into a lowland campsite, grabbed a five-year-old girl by the head and was dragging her away before the girl's father was able to beat it off with a large branch. As man's construction further en-croaches the natural habitat, attacks on humans increase. One day I'm driving a crew to a worksite in a van when we see a lion cross our path on the dirt road. It looks hungry; its ribs are showing.

But as it's always been, the most dangerous predator is man. There are several isolated campgrounds in the Ortegas. During one summer, an armed sex offender entered several family campsites and held a gun on one father while forcing the mom and daughter to perform oral sex. The potential for serious harm is always present.

I'm having an easy Sunday shift with my dorm. It's after break-fast and we're getting ready to watch football all day. Around the same time, Gary Alberts, one of the supervisors who lives in the trailer park, is in his pickup truck drinking coffee and smoking a cigarette at one of the scenic turnouts, just below Blue Jay Campground, which is a mile or so from Los Pinos. This is his Sunday morning ritual. He sees two young girls walking down the hill. He finishes his smoke, gets in his truck and is just about to pull out to head back when a blue Ford Ranger passes by on its way down the hill. Gary sees a white male driver wearing dark sunglasses, a camouflage baseball cap and jacket. He figures he's a deer hunter since the season is still open. He pulls out and starts heading home. As the truck ahead slowly drives past the girls, Gary hears gunshots and sees both girls fall to the ground. The truck speeds away. Gary frantically drives to the scene, places the girls in the back of his truck and drives to the trailer park. I get a call from the office telling me to lock the door and close all the curtains because there's been a shooting. The girls are dead. They were 12 years old and best friends. Their families have been camping together for years. Based on the vehicle description, partial plate number, and physical description Gary provides, law enforcement is able to identify the suspect. He's a middle-aged ex-Marine sharpshooter with survivalist training. They suspect he's still somewhere in the Cleveland National Forest. We're on lockdown trapped in our dorms.

On Monday morning, Von Roley decides the best plan of action is to go about business as usual. We line up in front of the office for the pre-breakfast head count. I look up at the hills surrounding the camp and wonder if the killer is up there looking at us. I've read that killers like to linger and return to the site of their murders. This is insane. And so it goes. The shooter is eventually located in Lake Elsinore, apprehended and successfully prosecuted, after leaving an everlasting black hole in the lives of two families.

I'm on a mission at Los Pinos to speak life into lives. Some days I run morning orientation where we gather the work crews into the rec hall and talk to them for a half-hour before starting the day. I talk my tough talk about my day, when there were no drive-bys, when you had to look your enemy in the eyes before battle, as if there was some romantic chivalry in it. It was still violent—with bats, bottles, chains, and knives—but it was close and intimate. I

23

sought to inspire some perspective, some thoughts toward understanding why they are killing each other, killing themselves.

MI HERMANOS
Why do we kill each other mi hermanos?
Because of territorial tradition,
Our macho condition,
The dusted coalition of our lives?

My skin is like yours.
Our streets are the same.
Our mothers wear the same black veils.
There are many closed doors.
We share the same pain.
They throw us in the same stinkin' jails.

But we keep crusin' round and round
over the same old ground.
You shoot my homeboy.
I pay back.
And they place another body on a cold steel rack.

We just drive by.
Our women cry.
But do we understand why?

We have all the excuses of our race,
all those things that keep us in our place:
Unemployment, poverty and liquor.
And that chiva is always the kicker!

We chant Viva la Raza
From a steel windowed casa
and tell ourselves we have pride.

We let our children pack
and shoot all that smack
then look for a place to hide.

We pray to the Holy Mother
then war with each other

wasting ourselves away

We speed through it all.
To our knees we fall.
Why are we so willing to pay?

The answer mi hermanos is inside us all
but we have to give up our hate.
Stop playing the role of the Vato Loco!
It's time to command your own fate!

Deputy Probation Counselor

With the Boys

"This is the verdict: Light has come into the world but men loved darkness instead of light because their deeds were evil." John 3:19 (NIV)

4

The Wedding

AND SO IT GOES . . . the Great Lopez California Migration continues.
My brother Steve flies out in August 1981 and stays with us for a
month until his first wife, Bobbie, arrives in September after driving cross-country. It's a very romantic story. Our families have been
close friends since we were kids. Mom and Barbara (Bobbie's mom)
met when they worked together on the Commack Volunteer Ambulance Corp. Bobbie has a younger sister, Lori, and a younger brother,
Chuck. The three are separated by a few years. We used to hang
out all the time at each other's homes. Bobbie and Lori have always
loved Steve and would spend the entire time chasing him around
the house. Bobbie and Steve move into a one-room apartment at
Calle las Bollas, in an old Spanish-style building near the beach a few
blocks away. The sink is in the middle of the living room. The other
residents are mostly Marines, which worries me a bit.

After a couple of months, they move into the four-unit building at 1002 Buena Vista. We live in apartment A, and they are in
D on the upper level. Bobbie and Steve both get jobs at McDonald's in San Clemente. She is quickly promoted to assistant manager and supervises Steve for three months, which inspires him to
seek employment elsewhere. He gets a job on the maintenance/
landscaping crew at the Dana Point Marina, where he works for
about a year before finding his first engineering job. Bobbie leaves
McDonald's and works as a special education teaching assistant in

the San Clemente school system. Our next-door neighbor from
Commack, Vinny St. Pierre, moves to San Clemente in '82. Bobbie
and Steve eventually get married on the bluff overlooking the Dana
Point Marina on July 24, 1982. Afterward, the reception is held at
a house where Vinny is living, overlooking a canyon. I carry in the
keg. Uncle George moves from New York City to L.A. in December
1983. We all followed my sister Teresa and our friends, Denise and
Mark, who caravanned cross-country in June of '79. We all live in
San Clemente but for Denise and Mark, who live in Dana Point in a
trailer park just up the coast.

And we're doing it. Paula is industrious. That first year, she
starts attending Saddleback Community College in Mission Viejo
while working two jobs. She waitresses at Howard Johnson's in San
Clemente, then the Jolly Roger at Dana Point Harbor. She finds her
"peeps" teaching three-year-olds at an affluent preschool in Laguna
Niguel. She tutors kids for a woman who runs a home-based special education program. She does the bills, cooks the food, does
the laundry, cleans the apartment, and makes breakfast, lunch, and
dinner. I think we're free, living with the ocean breeze, and don't
see that Paula is really sad and disconnected. Estranged from her
mother, she self medicates with weed and alcohol, and I'm blind to
the burden of the traditional role upon her life.

She's also my training partner at the gym, and we make love at
least twice a day, sometimes in exciting places like the beach. This
inspires me to write . . .

    T.V. Moonlight
    Cool silver
    T.V. moonlight
    loves you
    on the soft old couch.
    Your flesh glows
    like
      a
         fresh
             snow
                slope.
    My tongue

skis

down.

from areola
into
the light brown forest.

We get drunk together and smoke a little weed with Larry, our
good neighbor and friend from across the street.
He is a surfer dude, a skilled carpenter from Huntington
Beach. He is a sportsman. He surfs, skis, dives for lobsters at night,
goes spearfishing in the ocean for tuna, and goes four-wheeling in
the desert in his Toyota truck. He also lifts at the San Clemente
Health Club. He's about 5' 10," weighs around 200 pounds, and has
bushy blond hair and a thick mustache. He's barrel-chested and
benches 325. He's the embodiment of the Southern California man.
One winter day he starts out surfing at sunrise, goes four-wheeling
in the desert on his way to Big Bear Lake, snow skis at Big Bear,
and makes it back to end his day as it began— surfing— this time
at sunset. California is amazing. We call him "Larry Larry," a name
initiated by Uncle George who very much appreciated Larry.

We have our own little beach community on Buena Vista. We
look out for each other, party together, and help each other out.
Sometime in '82, Paula and I buy our new Toyota Tercel, a standard
five-speed. Larry Larry is also a car guy who can do anything, like
rebuild an engine. I know little to nothing. I want to change the
oil one day, and Larry and Steve volunteer to oversee the project
from a distance. They park themselves outside apartment D with
a 12-pack of Michelob and give me the thumbs up. I get under the
car, place the oil pan under the tank, unscrew the lid and drain it.
It looks a little too clear to me, but I get the thumbs up from my
supervisors when I question the viscosity. I finish the job and feel
satisfied. That night driving to a poetry reading in Mission Viejo,
the car sounds like a jet engine when I shift into fifth gear. It turns
out that I drained the transmission fluid and added four quarts of
oil. What's the cost of naïve ambition? What's the cost of a rebuilt
transmission?

Paula is the kindest, smartest, most beautiful person I know.
She's amazing. I'm madly in love with her and want to get married,

29

badly. My romantic warrior spirit has not yet fully matured, and so one day while soaking in some affectionate bliss, I say, "Hey, why don't we get married?" and she says, "We can't get married! We're not even engaged." So we get engaged. I spend a whopping $60 on a ring with a diamond chip. Our wedding doesn't cost much more.

We decide to offer our marriage as a gift to the Lord, marrying on the beach in San Clemente on December 25, 1981. I would not recommend this date for those newly engaged as the memory and celebration of your anniversary gets lost in the season. We write our own vows. I come up with a rhyme scheme and somehow get in a reference to the zoo and our favorite animals. In addition to her vows, Paula also writes a short sermon on love to be read by the pastor. She is taking a philosophy course at the time. She writes about the power of love and starts talking about "Victor Frankel, a man who was forced to live in Nazi concentration camps as a child, forced to march in the snow from one camp to another; this is a man who could talk of love. . ." I convince her that her vows would have some of our guests suffering and wondering about her sanity, and we do a little editing. Paula designs the invitations, which say: "I can only find freedom in the ropes that bind me to you." I wonder if people are going to think we might be into a little bondage. My parents don't come because Paula's parents won't be there. She's been disowned by her mother, Gloria, who's still not talking to her. A week before the wedding, she calls Paula and tells her that if she marries on Christmas, she will ruin that day for the rest of Gloria's life. I don't really think much about this, about the pain and anguish in Paula's heart. I just think about us. I just want to get married.

Our guest list includes: Teresa and Brad; Bobbie and Steve; Larry Larry; Mack, my supervisor from Los Pinos, with his wife and daughter; Phil, a counselor from the camp, with Chris, one of the youthful wards of the state; Tommy, a beach bum from San Clemente just released from Los Pinos; Bruce, another counselor; and Mark and Denise, who know an ordained minister who works full-time as a rodeo clown. I get ready at our apartment in the company of Steve, Mark, and Tommy. Meanwhile, Paula is with my sister at her place.

I'm wearing a white shirt with white slacks from a local consignment shop on Del Mar. Paula finds the perfect wedding "gown" at the Santa Ana Flea Market for $13. Our wedding site is on the beach about halfway between 204 and the pier. We pick low tide because there are large rocks near the shore that Paula and I love to wade out to. The men and I head off to the wedding, down the stairs to the beach and toward the pier. We're walking, four men, side-by-side, Steve on my right, Mark on my left, and Tommy next to Mark. We're marching in the sand, stride-by-stride, when Steve starts whistling the tune from one of our favorite movies, *The Good, The Bad, and The Ugly*, and Mark declares that we are "the good, the bad, and the married."

We arrive at the spot. Our guests are arriving. There's a parking lot right there and a bluff on either side. For some reason unknown, Brad drops Paula off at the top of the bluff, and she has to scale down the steep hill. I see her up above, standing straight and tall, her golden hair artfully braided in a Baby's Breath wreath. She descends, gracefully, carefully placing each step. Still, I'm afraid she might lose her footing and fall. She makes it unscathed yet a little out of breath. She looks like a medieval princess bride. Our guests surround us, and the rodeo clown starts the ceremony. There are joggers running and families walking by, pausing to see the wedding on Christmas Day on the beach. We exchange vows and sing a duet, "With You I'm Born Again" by Billy Preston and Syreeta. *"Come show me your kindness. In your arms I know I'll find this. . . I was half not whole, in step with none, reaching through this world in need of one. . ."*

We are pronounced husband and wife and turn to walk into the ocean. But I'm stuck for a moment; I look down to see that my feet are buried in the sand up to my ankles. We stand on the rocks and watch the waves. The reception is on the patio at our apartment. We have wine and beer and our guests bring food. Paula cooks her first turkey in the oven in a brown paper bag, but in the imbibing we forget about it and find it the next morning still in the paper bag, still in the oven. Bobbie and Steve bring the cake, and I end up wearing most of it on my face when we cut the first slice for Paula to serve. We dance and drink and eat as the night goes on, but I know Paula is sad because no one in her family is here. I am tempted and go on a coke run with Tommy. Not a great way to begin my husbandry, and a low moment in my professional career. We come up empty. The entire wedding costs us 240 bucks. And we are married. And so it goes. And a sonnet now and then helps stir our romance.

THE BEAUTY OF YOUR EYES
If I could write the beauty of your eyes,
such verse would sing the essence of my love.
These lines in time would reach eternal skies
of dawn's first rays of light to stars above.
If I could write the wonders of your mind
No book could ever bind the depth of thought.
I'd search and reach and grasp what I could find
And hold in close the knowledge that was caught.
If I could write the music of your praise,
God's worshipers would have a holy song,
to learn and sing and dance through all our days,
for peace and joy to rain and make us strong.
If I could write the beauty of your eyes,
such verse would I first see each time I rise.

"Submit to one another out of reverence for Christ." Ephesians 5:21
(NIV)

5

Gloria Days

MOM IS STILL WORKING the graveyard shift at the Huntington Hospital Emergency Room. Her friends call her "RN Mary," which is also on her license plate. During one shift in February 1982, she sees a name she recognizes in triage . . . Gloria Gill, Paula's mom. She hasn't met Paula's parents. She reads the chart and sees that Paula's dad, Bill Gill, brought her in because she has lost a lot of weight and is lethargic. Gloria is being prepped for emergency surgery because she has severe ulcerative colitis; her intestines have burst and she needs an ileostomy to save her life, which requires the removal of her small intestines. She only weighs 80 pounds and is very weak. Mom goes directly to Gloria's room and sees a middle-aged man leaning against the wall, reading the New York Times. She approaches him, "Hello Mr. Gill? I'm Mary Lopez, Ray's mother." "Who?" "Ray's mother. Ray Lopez, your son-in-law." "Oh, hello! It's nice to meet you."

Paula's parents have a terrible marriage mangled by Bill's alcoholism and intermittent unemployment. Gloria's prognosis is very poor. Colitis is caused by stress. Ironically, the primary cause of her stress also saved her life. Had Bill not brought Gloria to the ER that day, she would've died at home.

Gloria makes it through surgery and is placed in the ICU. Mom calls Paula and tells her, "Your mom is really sick. You should come home and say goodbye." Paula and Gloria haven't talked since we moved to California. The day before we left New York, Paula went home to pack some clothes and found every trace of her existence in bags on the curb at the end of the driveway. She went into her room and found it bare but for a few tacks on the wall. She flies to New York immediately. When she first walks into her mom's hospital room, she sees a tiny head on a pillow in a large bed. Gloria sees her and smiles. She is skin and bones. Paula talks to the doctor; he tells her that Gloria is day-to-day but very weak and not likely to survive. She tells him that her mom's a very strong woman. Back in San Clemente, I'm hanging out with Tommy. We get drunk every day. I'm still enslaved by alcohol.

I call Paula on Valentine's Day and play our wedding song, "With You I'm Born Again," on the turntable in the background. Mostly we share sobs and I'm a blubbering slob. She sees her mom every day and at night hangs out with my old training partner, Steve Deluca, who's still bouncing at Good Times. I think Mom has finally forgiven him for hiring me as a bouncer back in the day. Paula plans to stay until Gloria is in full recovery mode. She knows that the stress of her leaving home added fuel to her mother's disease. But she is healing, and the doctors call it a miracle. Paula's there for two weeks in total. On the day of her departure, she drops her little sister, Carla, off at school. They hug each other in the lobby of Burr Junior High School, and neither wants to let go.

Gloria makes a full recovery and starts her new life with an ileostomy bag. That Christmas, Paula and I return to Commack. We go back and forth between our parents' homes, which is exhausting. I am still an infant Christian, drinking spiritual milk when I think about it and praying only when I'm scared. And I'm still drinking and smoking weed. My old demons are lurking in the dark, waiting for the right moment to strike. They attack the night before our flight back to L.A. in Paula's old bedroom. We are tired from the emotional trip, and I can't fall asleep. I finally start to doze off around 3 a.m. when it comes.

I'm suddenly jerked awake and see a reddish vapor at the foot of the bed. It starts moving toward me, and I'm trapped in a moment of terror. I'm in the dark, but I fight back. I jump on top of the demon, pin it down and just as I'm about to reign down hammer fists, I see that it's Paula beneath me. The deceiver flees as Paula throws me to the floor. A second wave of terror rushes through as she tries to comfort me in my agony. She is brave and unharmed. It's a good thing she has such strong legs. This will not be the last attack. Our demons follow us, and wait . . . this is the beginning of the whisper of fear I hear before I fall asleep each night wondering . . .

Dad drives us to JFK later that day and drops us off in front of the departure terminal. I know he's proud of me. He hugs Paula goodbye, then turns to me and says, "Ray, you're the head of the family now." I'm drained and still feeling the edges of shock from my battle that morning. I can't think of anything to say but "Okay dad. I love you." We exchange a quick macho hug and we're off. In the Latino culture the oldest son is responsible to lead the family, but Dad is 51 and will live another 36 years. I'm far from being the head of the family but close to understanding what he is trying to tell me. I need to grow up, get my shit together and get ready.

"When I was a child, I talked like a child, I thought like a child, I reasoned like a child. When I became a man, I put the ways of childhood behind me." 1 Corinthians 13:11 (NIV)

6

Mexico

MEXICO IS CALLING ME from southern winds, from brown families working the fields, from smells wafting out of cocinas, from memories of my Abuela's mole sauce and enchiladas, from Spanish tiles on the rooftops, from music, from my mind's echo of my Abuela singing the sweet songs and my dad and uncles belting out *Rancho Grande*. And we go to Mexico.

Driving south on I-5 you start seeing signs of desperate lives just past San Diego, traffic signs alerting drivers to watch out for humans crossing the freeway, like you see deer-crossing signs in the Catskills. These lives tend to sneak up on you at times, like the day Paula and I drive up to the haunted graveyard above the old mission in San Juan Capistrano. There are hundreds of unmarked graves of the Indians who heard the Gospel from the Spanish missionaries and built the famous mission with adobe bricks. As we reach the top of the hill in our black van, we see a dozen young Mexican men drop to the ground. They remain frozen as we drive slowly by, make a U-turn and leave.

A couple of years later, we're sitting in our new 1985 red Toyota mini-pickup truck in the parking lot looking down at the San Clemente Pier. The train track runs along the coast. It sits on a steep levy to avoid flooding from storms. We're drinking coffee and enjoying the sun and the ocean breeze when a few young Mexican men come out of nowhere, climb over the tracks and approach me on the driver's side of the truck. Their leader gives me a piece of paper with a local address written on it. My Spanish is good enough for me to say, "No," then quickly pull out and drive away. Paula wants to know why I didn't give them a ride. We both have a lot to learn.

We do our Christmas shopping in Tijuana. We park the van and walk across the border. The Mexican authorities just look you over as you walk by. It's very sad to see the economic disparity; breastfeeding mothers beg on the street with children beside them; street kids run up and surround you with open hands and puppy eyes. The 1%, who own 99% of the wealth, built the outdoor shopping mall. It is opulent, displaying finely laid cement structures with walls of pink, salmon, and light brown; stone walkways and water fountains abound. You can find similar malls in Irvine or Costa Mesa. In Tijuana you barter. I'm feeling quite competent in my Spanglish as I haggle with a teenage boy over the price of some leather bags. And I know he's won when he says "Chingada tu madre" and walks back into the store, where his mother is not looking very happy. I pay him the price he's asking.

Going to Mexico is easy. Coming back not so much. A Mexican-American with a New York accent driving a large black van with a green-eyed blonde as a passenger will draw special attention from the U.S. Border Patrol. Our typical stop would involve a lengthy interview and thorough search underneath and around the vehicle with optimal illumination of the interior, seeking cause for a warrantless search. On average we were held up for at least 45 minutes, but it was always worth it.

We take some more adventurous trips with Larry Larry. In Orange County you see a lot of people wearing "Hussong's Cantina, Ensenada" t-shirts, and you hear a lot of stories. Just two hours south of the border, it is the mecca of partying for Marines, college kids, surfers, and rogues. We frequent Hussong's on occasion. On return trips we stop off at Rosarita Beach, which is halfway between Ensenada and the border. There are small beachfront restaurants where we eat fresh lobster tails. There's also a stylish casino and hotel that was built by L.A. gangsters in the 1920s, where we have dinner and watch mariachi shows with flamenco dancers. Some of the stories are cautionary, like people waking up lying naked in an alley, or in a police cell. You call who you can to get money, sent via Western Union, to pay the police to be released. The locals are very friendly at Hussong's.

On one trip with Larry Larry, we party with reckless abandon and are caught up in the pandemonium when we realize that Paula is missing! The revelation that she is gone is sobering, and we frantically search the nearby streets. In a moment of near panic, out of the corner of my eye, I see a flash of blonde in a sea of brown down a street a few blocks away. We take off in a sprint calling out "Paula!" As we close in, we see that it's her, but she keeps walking off to nowhere. We catch up and find that she is fine, just walking through a blackout on a sunny day in Ensenada. But for God's great mercy on that day she might have not returned to California.

"Blessed are the merciful for they shall obtain mercy."
Matthew 5:7 (NIV)

7

The Drinking Game

THERE ARE WAYS TO measure addiction in small moments, like emptying the Incredible Hulk bank—that Paula bought me as a gift—to find enough change for a box of wine, or selling your collection of 100 vinyl LPs for 50 bucks . . . which buys a couple of cases of Michelob and a few bottles of cheap wine. We had it all, from Beethoven to Hendrix, most in mint condition.

I come from a long line of highly functional alcoholics. My Dad, for example, the inventor of the Lopez Feed, which students read about in textbooks on electrical engineering, has 50 patents in his name and was awarded the highest honors in his field. A highly functional drunk is very organized, unless they have executive functioning deficits, which I do not. The top priority of each day is to plan and secure the daily alcohol ration.

On a normal day, I must first determine if there is an adequate supply of beer and wine, and then casually think about the rest of the day. Working out always comes first, then a nap on the weekends, and then after a protein-filled lunch, the drinking begins. Ironically, other than the massive alcohol consumption, we are living healthy lives with plenty of exercise and a good diet. Otherwise, if it's a scheduled event, like a concert or some other social gathering, it must first be established whether there will be alcohol present in order to determine whether you should bring your own. If it is a venue where alcohol is prohibited, you must either drink an adequate amount before, or preferably, scheme a way to bring in the booze, undetected, and drink fast, undetected. Achieving this criteria brings with it not only a feeling of peace, but also excitement. And intellectualizing. I don't drink every day. I don't drink at work. I am highly motivated to finish my shift on that third day by the thought of the 6-pack I will finish off on the drive down the mountain. I can drive drunk and have only been pulled over twice.

The first time, Paula and I decide it's a great idea to get a case of beer, throw it in a cooler with ice and take an evening drive down to Oceanside. We finish off a few before our departure. Oceanside is about 20 miles south of San Clemente. We get down there, drive through the center of town to see what's happening, and I get pulled over by Oceanside cops. They say I drove through a red light, smell alcohol on my breath, and ask me to get out of the car to complete a sobriety test. I follow the finger, touch my nose, say the alphabet (forward, thank God), and as I begin the heel-to-toe walk of balance, Paula leans out the window and starts cheering me on, just like we're back in high school on the football field. "Ray Lopez, he's our man. If he can't do it nobody can!" This is quite irresponsible of her, and she is appropriately reprimanded by the officer with a threat of arrest should she fail to cease and desist as ordered. I'm in the zone. I pass and receive a ticket for going through a red light. The officers do not look inside the cooler Paula is sitting on and do not find the remains of our case of beer thrown casually in back of the van.

Another night I'm driving down "The Highway of Death" after a staff party at the trailer park above Los Pinos. By this time we have purchased a new 1985 Honda CRX. It has rack-and-pinion steering, and I'm loving leaning into those snaky curves so the wheels screech enough to let you know you're at maximum speed. Back in town, I'm a little more relaxed, and we're close to home when I see the flashing lights in the rearview mirror and pull over. I hand over my license, registration, and proof of insurance along with my county ID, which has my photo and esteemed title, Deputy Probation Counselor. I'm looking for a little law enforcement love. He's San Clemente PD and tells me that he's seen me around town. He tells me I was weaving all over the road, that I'm a fool for risking my wife's life, and that I'm in no condition to drive. He knows we're just a couple of blocks from home and tells me to take it slow and lets me go. I can drive drunk fine. I'm just a little tired. That's all. It's been a long day.

Now, it's true that steady, well-balanced intoxication can affect certain physical activities. I learn this one night while bodysurfing. I'm alone, which isn't great, but it seems like a good idea at the time. After a few attempts, I catch that wave that picks you up and propels you forward like a torpedo, with speed and the fury of the wave in your ears. I'm riding this wave when it folds under, and I see that I am about to be planted, face first, into the rocky sand below me. In a breath I tuck my head and roll through to my feet! Had I been less of an athlete, I would've broken my neck. It was exhilarating. Steady, well-balanced intoxication can affect certain physical activities.

Alcohol can inspire artistic vision. One night me, Paula, Bobbie, and Steve are out on the deck enjoying some beer and wine. I'm the barbeque chef. I know by the number of beers I drink when the chicken is done. A 6-pack will ensure there's not a trace of pink in the meat. I keep the hedges down to enhance our ocean view, but in between the condos across the street some trees have been planted, partially obstructing the scene. This bothers me, and Steve agrees that it's bullshit. Later that night, Steve and I decide to free the ocean breeze. There are two trees doing the damage. Steve has his trusty foldable Boy Scout saw and at midnight, we cross the street and swiftly cut the trees down. The next morning we're on the patio drinking coffee and staring at the whitecaps from our newly improved view. The landscaping guy arrives and is upset and dismayed the trees he planted have been cut down. He sees us and shares his concerns. He asks if we heard anything last night or saw any suspicious characters. We respond in the negative. He shakes his head and says, "Man, that's fucked up. This sucks." We nod, take a sip of coffee watching the waves coming in and agree, "Yea man. That's really fucked up. People are such assholes."

Such highly functional, artistic visionary drinking involves sacrifices. What's a couple of trees, numerous blackouts, and a few nights wetting the bed? Paula also has a drinking problem, and she's a codependent. She's concerned that I'm drinking too much but is willing to play the numbers game. You have to stay on top of it, but you need to keep enough beer and wine in the fridge to create the illusion that you're not drinking as much. Whereas you might've drank a 12-pack of beer on a Saturday, instead you drink a 6-pack and enough glasses of wine (large bottles are essential, but boxes are best) to get to the same place. It looks like you've had less to drink. I learned this during my adolescence by going through my parents' fully stocked liquor cabinet. If I took shots from different bottles they didn't notice. Part of the codependent's identity is linked with their role, which eventually supports the ongoing drinking with expressed concern of over-consumption. Under the right circumstances this duality can extend for long periods of time until tragedy arrives. The codependent joins the illusion of the numbers game, actually receiving some small comfort while knowing nothing has really changed.

On November 21, 1983, Paula's maternal grandfather, Thomas O'Neil, goes to be with the Lord. She is heartbroken, devastated, and we are 3000 miles away. I should've stayed with her that night, comforted her like a good husband. But instead, I go off to watch the first Leonard/Duran fight with some buddies from work. The whole night's a blackout for me. The sun in my face awakens me the next morning. I find myself laying on the kitchen floor covered in Doritos. (Paula was so upset that I left her alone that night that she went out to the Fish Tale, a local restaurant/bar, and partied with five Marines whom she drove back to Camp Pendleton. When she came home around 2 a.m., she found me sitting there, wasted, stuffing my face with Doritos. I wasn't even concerned where she had been. Enraged, she grabbed the bag out of my hands and voraciously pummeled me with it.

Like all my blackouts, I quickly expel the moment of fear and panic and pick myself up off the floor. It's Monday morning and I have to be at work by 2:30 that afternoon. I open the refrigerator, remove a bottle of red and pour myself a glass. I've never done this before! Paula's in the bedroom sleeping. I sit on the floor in front of the window so I can lift the glass and watch the rays of the sun pass through it, illuminating the wine, giving it fire. I do this all the time.

But I feel the presence of the Lord in my heart and hear the voice of the enemy in my mind. And I'm taken back to my days in the psych hospital when God first heard my heart cry and gave me the power to wrestle with the devil, pin him to the mat and rise. And I see the fire of hell in that glass leading to death. I've been drinking for 14 years, and I'm only 24! I feel a sharp pain in my side, like the Apostle Paul who ". . . was given a thorn in my flesh, a messenger of Satan, to torment me." 2 Corinthians 12:7. I put the glass down.

We drive up the mountain in silence that afternoon. Stan Wolfe is the best counselor at Los Pinos and he's a recovering alcoholic. He sees that I look like shit and can smell the booze still oozing through my pores. He knows and stays close to me for the next three days. He helps me to see the truth, that I am a slave, in bondage, an alcoholic. I stop drinking. This saves our marriage, and the pain in my side subsides after a couple weeks.

"But he said to me, 'My grace is sufficient for you, for my power is made perfect in weakness.'" 2 Corinthians 12:9 (NIV)

8

College

PAULA AND I ARE taking courses at Saddleback Community College in Mission Viejo. She starts in the Spring '81 semester, and I start in the fall. I'm still working the weekend shift at Los Pinos, so I have the entire week to go to school and I make the best of it. It's free for California residents, defined as one who has lived in the state for a year. Paula's New York driver's license was lost in the ocean, so she has a California license and they let her enroll without any questions. She looks like a California girl. We sometimes get a kick out of it like when we went to the Mann's Chinese Theatre in L.A., where the Hollywood Walk of Fame is, and some Chinese tourists ask to take a picture with her. She also looks like a movie star.

So when I start out, I'm thinking it makes sense to take courses that will complement my professional career like counseling and juvenile justice; I'm also receiving 40 hours a year of professional training from the county, so it's very redundant. I could ace all my courses with a major in Criminal Justice, but I'm bored. I love literature, and I still consider myself somewhat of a poet. I read my first book, *Dr. Jekyll and Mr. Hyde,* by Robert Louis Stevenson, when I was seven years old. My second book was *Journey to the Center of the Earth* by Jules Verne. Majoring in English is wonderful. You have to learn the classics, follow the *golden thread,* and recognize the allusions that run through the centuries. You have to become a critical reader. Most English majors focus on British and American Lit.

How hard is it to determine whether *Moby Dick* or *Huck Finn* is the greatest American novel? I know it's a short list. Yes, Twain deals with the societal issue of the time that was tearing the country apart—slavery—and in that respect, it's as real as it can be . . . and timeless. In contrast, the lyricism of his writing when Huck and Jim are together on the raft going down the Mississippi is beautiful. They are free to love one another like brothers and see each other's heart. But I'm a champion of Literary Realism, and Melville writes all of us onto the Pequod as passengers. Although the character development in the first 100 pages is familiar and at times quite humorous, once you get on that ship you are Melville's prisoner, just like the crew held captive by Ahab's megalomaniacal pursuit of the whale. The reader struggles through the minutia of each chapter, like the one on cooking whale blubber, or sharpening a harpoon, or 19th-century navigational instruments. But you have to keep reading until the whale shows up. Mercifully, the chapters are short, but you don't get to see *Moby Dick* until you're about 300 pages in. This monotonous boredom is the life of a 19th-century whaler. It is a bummer of an ending because we have only seen the whale twice before *Moby Dick* surfaces again, sinks the ship, and the crew is killed, except for Ishmael.

And for you Huck fans, which was first published in 1884, I venture to say that Twain was strongly influenced by Melville's *Moby Dick*, published in 1851, in his development of Tom Sawyer's character. Just as Ahab uses his crew for his maniacal purposes by tempting them with gold to overcome their fears, Tom uses Huck, abuses Jim, and nearly drives his Aunt Sally and Uncle Silas insane when he forces Huck and Jim to go along with his fantastical schemes to break Jim out of captivity. Tom only cares about satisfying his desire to playact his great adventure. Like Ahab, Tom is truly insane. Like the crew of the Pequod and Ahab, Huck and Jim are mesmerized by the force of Tom's presence and imagination. He spends weeks concocting the nonsensical details of Jim's several escape attempts, even though Jim could've been freed the very first night. The key to the shed was hanging in the kitchen in plain sight. On the night of the escape, Tom nearly gets the three of them killed. But nobody dies, and Tom doesn't lose a leg, even though he receives a bullet wound to his calf. English is a great major.

Saddleback is an excellent college. I do the general education requirements and otherwise take courses in Creative Writing in Poetry, Intro to Film, Observational Astronomy (which satisfies the lab requirement) and my favorites, Intro to Science Fiction I and II. Paula and I even write a short story together, "Mind Maneuvers," a tale of scientists who create life in a lab in Arizona by projecting holographic images into the minds of severely intellectually disabled test subjects. I take full credit for it in class, and Professor Campbell says it's as good as the early short stories of Arthur C. Clarke. *Amazing Science Fiction Stories* rejects the story because it ". . . does little more, at bottom, than to reveal a wonder; and there is far, far too much explanation; also 'idiot lecture' ("As you already know. . ."). Some of the science is fine but some is not." Well, looking ahead, revealing a wonder is what we need, and the debate about good and bad science will frame the end of the world.

I end up with 90 credits from Saddleback, and Paula graduates with an associate degree in early childhood education. We both begin attending Cal State Fullerton and pay $250 a semester. I'm able to transfer 70 credits, more than halfway to my degree. I'm still loving my major, doing Milton, Shakespeare ("Out damn spot!"), and American and British Poetry. Paula, after 10 years, attending four colleges in two states on two coasts finally settles on psychology as her last of four attempted majors and graduates with her BA from Cal State Fullerton Magna Cum Laude in December 1985.

We become part of The Laguna Beach Poets scene. We do Open Mic Night; I get a few poems published in *Electrum and California Quarterly,* and I'm even the featured poet one Friday night. My stuff is street and lockup. Gregory Corso comes to my reading and sits in the back of the room. He's the featured reader the next night. As I read my poems, he sways with his eyes closed, rocking his head up and down to the beat and rhythm of my lines, or so I believe. We all party together afterward, and he tells me he likes my stuff and that I should send him a manuscript. I never send him anything, but I see him again in a documentary on Kerouac.

A Poem in a Dream
a poem in a dream
words in my hand
lines with rhythm
wonderfully written
my best work
                              yet
when I wake it is gone

nothing, nada not even a tone.
I search my brain
    wait   concentrate
for what?
maybe it wasn't me
                              but
some dead unpublished poet
automatic writing
in the synapse of my night.

I watch T.V. instead.
there I find Corso
snarling through a documentary
on Kerouac about knowing
whether or not you're a poet
and living in denial
like some junky
or seeing something
no one else has
and writing it.

a poet in a dream
after a reading
talking to a beautiful young blond
woman about the passion and erotica
in my work
then her flesh decomposes
down to the bone.
when I wake I think of all
those horror movies.

a poet in a dream

Sylvia Plath and her daughter
are staying at our house.
They have long full blonde hair
that falls together as they roll
around the living room wrestling
laughing. she loves my poems
wants to help   but
I have to go to work.
when I come home they are gone
without a forwarding address.

when I wake I read her journal.
in it she wrote,
"To be god:
to be every life before we die:
a dream to drive men mad."

a poem in a dream
a dream in a poem
it's all one

come home
watch T.V
watch the food cook

            in the oven

sit on the bowl
read
sometimes I write it.

After Paula graduates with her BA, she applies for graduate
school. We're doing well. It's been two years since we had a drink.
She gets accepted into the School Psychology PhD program at
Berkeley! We are thrilled and there's a huge shift in our lives. Now
all the focus is on her. It's always been on me because of my interesting job and my poetry. Our family and friends are very excited, and
after congratulating Paula and talking about the school and the Bay
Area, some turn to me and ask, "And, what are you going to do,
Ray?" We move to the Bay Area in August 1986.

Take fast hold of instruction; let *her* not go: keep her; for she *is* thy life.
Proverbs 4:13 (KJV)

9

Bezerkely

OUR FIRST APARTMENT IS in the basement of a house up in Kensington with a gorgeous view of the bay. We eventually move into Albany Village, a student-housing complex just north of Berkeley up the I-80. It's an old Army family apartment track. I have to take a weekend shift at Los Pinos so I have the week free to go to school and look for a new job. I leave my truck with my sister in San Clemente and fly out of Oakland Airport every Friday night. It's an hour flight. Teresa picks me up at John Wayne Airport in Santa Ana; I sleep at her apartment, then drive up the mountain early Saturday morning. I start taking courses at Cal State Hayward (now Cal State East Bay) just south of Oakland. I commute for the next eight months, until I am hired by the Contra Costa County Probation Department as a group counselor at the Boys' Treatment Center in Martinez. My time as a commuter came with some adventures in the air.

On October 8, 1986, I'm waiting to fly home in the Southwest Airline terminal at John Wayne Airport one Monday afternoon when Reggie Jackson just strolls in, wearing blue jeans, cowboy hat, boots, and a leather vest. He's been with the Angels since 1982. The day before, one pitch away from going to World Series, Angels pitcher Donnie Moore gave up a game-winning home run to Dave Henderson of the Boston Red Sox. The Sox ended up losing to my New York Mets thanks to Bill Buckner's infamous error at first base during Game Six. Donnie Moore committed suicide on July 18, 1989. Baseball can be a tough game. So Reggie's in the terminal, and people are keeping a safe distance but for one brave little boy who manages to get an autograph. We board the small single-aisle plane and I'm sitting about halfway down. Reggie is the last passenger to board, and he starts walking toward the back of the plane. I can't believe it's Reggie Jackson, and I can't take my eyes off him. During my most peaceful moments, I look like I'm angry, and I haven't yet learned Philippians 4: 5 that teaches to "Let your gentleness be evident to all." We lock eyes and Reggie looks pissed, but I can't stop staring. As he passes by, he keeps glaring back and his eyes are saying to me, "What the fuck are you looking at?" When Paula picks me up in Oakland, I tell her "I think I almost got into a fight on the plane with Reggie Jackson!"

The next week it's *déjà vu all over again* at John Wayne. Reggie's in the terminal but the mood is entirely different. There are rumors abounding that he will be returning to the Oakland A's for his final season, and he's smiling and entertaining a bunch of A's fans. Once we board, Reggie is again the last one on and exchanges pleasantries with passengers as he walks down the aisle. Paula meets me in the terminal in Oakland, and I excitedly tell her that Reggie was on the plane again. We sit in the terminal and wait. He gets off about fifteen minutes after the plane is empty and starts walking toward the exit. As he passes by, I call out, "Hey Reggie! Looking good, man." He says, "Thanks man," and gives me a thumbs up. Me and Reggie, we're good.

The Bay Area is notorious for its fog, and planes can get stacked deep when there isn't enough visibility to land safely. The smaller planes don't carry that much fuel and will sometimes have to return to Orange County, where everybody scrambles to get a standby return flight. It can get nasty, and this happens to me a few times during the months I commute. One day it took me seven hours to fly back to the Bay Area. On the flight there, we're scheduled to be in a holding pattern for about an hour, so the pilot decides to continue to Portland to drop off passengers with that final destination. On the way back we end up in another holding pattern, so the pilot decides to continue south to drop off the Monterey passengers we picked up in Portland and offers to drop off the Oakland passengers in Monterrey as well, because he will now have to return to Orange County to refuel and people can try to get a flight from Monterrey back to Oakland. I'm not getting off the plane. We land at John Wayne and I have to get another flight. Meanwhile, Paula's been at Oakland Airport trying to get information to find out where I am. When I finally get off the plane in Oakland, she hugs me like there's no tomorrow. She thought I might have gotten off in Monterrey, fell off the wagon and was sitting in a bar in a drunken state. And so it goes.

The Bay Area is the best place we have ever lived. Walking down Telegraph Avenue is like walking through a time portal into the 1960s. Most people think of Selma, Alabama, and Rosa Parks, but People's Park is arguably where the Civil Rights Movement started. There is a large middle-class minority population; walk into any public or private school classroom and you'll find a good mix of Black, White, Hispanic, and Asian students. The University is beautiful. You have to walk through Sather Gate to get to Wheeler Hall, where the English department is. Sather Tower is prominent, and Memorial Stadium sits on a hill to the east overlooking the campus and University Avenue, stretching to the Bay. We often sit in Lower Sproul Plaza drinking cappuccinos from the Milano Café, listening to the weekend percussionists play in front of Zellerbach Hall, watching the street dancers move with the beat, the undergrads getting drunken loud at the Golden Bear, Frisbees flying with the smell of marijuana in the air.

In the late 80s, the City of Berkeley is still a hot spot of activism, but the University is very conservative. One day Paula and I are sitting across from Sproul Hall, the administration building. As usual, we're drinking our cappuccinos before going to the rec center to work out. There's a large crowd of students with picket signs protesting apartheid. A suit comes out with a megaphone and tells the crowd that they can't block the entrance to the building and must disperse or the campus police will have to remove them. There are lots of steps leading up to the front entrance. The students get louder. We're just sipping our coffee, taking it all in. About a dozen campus cops exit the building, make a line at the top of the steps and descend without warning—raising their nightsticks to strike. And they crush the kids who turn to escape, screaming like they're running from Godzilla. It's crazy. People are down on the ground crying; some are being handcuffed, some are being chased out onto Durant Avenue, which borders the south side of the University. Paula and I finish our cappuccinos and start heading to the gym, and I think to myself, *those kids would've been better off in class.* Clearly I did not come of age in the 60s.

We absorb the East Bay and San Francisco like sea sponges. We walk along Jack London Square and take the Bart into the city, doing the tourist thing: Pier 39, Alcatraz, Coit Tower, Lombard Street, Chinatown, Golden State Park, North Beach, Cliff House, the Golden Gate Bridge, Sausalito, and the giant Redwoods of Muir Woods. But we love Haight-Ashbury, and the City Lights Bookstore is the mecca for those who see their literary lineage in the beat poets. We are suddenly a very popular visiting destination for our relatives, and over time we become accomplished amateur tour guides, taking our guests off the scenic route. We eventually perfect the "Six Bridge" tour of the Bay Area—never having to pay a toll.

Our lives have never been fuller. Paula is immersed in her doctoral program and working in the Evaluation Unit in Tollman Hall, the home of the School of Education and the School Psychology program, on the far north side of campus. I'm working a crazy shift at the Boys' Treatment Center: Monday, 7 a.m. to 3 p.m.; Tuesday, 3 p.m. to 11p.m.; Wednesday, the same as Monday; and Thursday through Friday, 3 p.m. to 7 a.m. The boys at the Center are wards of the court, serving out sentences from six months up to a year. They're hardcore, just like the guys at Los Pinos, with multiple convictions for robbery, arson, narcotics, weapons, sexual assault, and so it goes. Ninety-five percent of our residents are Black and Hispanic, and most are from Richmond, the home of Shell Oil and a diverse population. The students of Richmond High School speak 26 different languages, accounting for the numerous dialects of families from Southeast Asia and Central America. Richmond has a population of approximately 100,000, as compared to nearly half a million in Oakland, which has a well-deserved reputation as a tough city. Statistically, Richmond is much worse. There's an unincorporated section, North Richmond, which is patrolled by a couple of Highway Patrol units. It's no-man's land, with one way in and one way out. There are numerous Asian and Latino gangs competing for the corner markets. We buy our first home in Richmond.

The Boys' Center is described as a maximum-security therapeutic facility, a real oxymoron. It's self-contained. Only the staff goes in and out. Our residents eat, sleep, shower, work, and go to school, all within the Center. These guys are one step away from a bed in the California Youth Authority (CYA), a juvenile prison system, which holds the worst of the worst until they parole at the age of 21. A kid can be convicted of murder when he's 15 and be paroled six years later, unless he catches another case in the CYA and graduates to the California Department of Corrections—which has some of the worst prisons in the country like San Quentin, across the Bay, just over the Richmond-San Raphael Bridge.

The Boys' Center is an intimate setting, and we get very close to our charges. There's a supervisor and two counselors during the day shift, two counselors for the swing and one to work the graveyard. There are five cells with two beds in each, down two cold hallways on opposite sides of the counselors' station. The bathrooms are near the day room, which leads out into the small courtyard with one basketball hoop. You have to love it or you will become part of the problem. We do some good work, go into some deep stuff, and there is some healing. At times, we have to physically restrain a kid who's being violent. We're trained to apply painful arm bars and wrist holds that are very effective. There are kids with serious mental health problems who need time to calm down. In rare instances, we would place a young man on his steel frame bed and apply soft ties to each limb.

Family is still involved because the painful reality is that if they make it out, they go back to the same scene. Toward that end, guys who are programming successfully earn home visits and get searched when they return. We're always looking for drugs and weapons. One weekend we avoid a nightmare when we find a dozen hits of acid sewed into the tongue of this kid's sneakers. He tells us that he was waiting for his next shift on kitchen duty and was planning to drop the acid into the punch we serve at lunchtime. We eat together, staff and residents, and we all like the tropical punch. Dodged multiple hits on that potential disaster.

I'm still loving school but this new schedule with work and classes is stretching me. I meet Professor Don Markos at Hayward. He loves William Carlos Williams and teaches poetry and short story workshops. He's a wonderful mentor. I meet the works of Chaucer and Milton, add courses in Mythology and Music Listening to boost my GPA, and start thinking in Spanish in Conversational Spanish 2. I graduate with my B.A. in English on June 13, 1987. On my final day, I go straight from work to school. In order to satisfy the mandatory second language requirement for English majors, I translate a speech by Batista . . . and I'm done! I'm feeling good and satisfied. When I get home, I step inside the front door, take a second step, collapse onto the couch running a 102-degree fever and sleep for three days. It's amazing what you can do when you're young.

I apply to the English master's program at Cal. I do terribly on the GRE, as I know nothing about Chinese literature. I start freaking out and go to see the chair of the English Department to seek advice about retaking the exam. He tells me it isn't important and starts talking about the high intelligence of pigs. I get out of there quickly and figure I have nothing to worry about. I get in. Affirmative Action is still a thing and not yet declared a failed social experiment. But I have a cumulative GPA of 3.74, so maybe my last name didn't have too much to do with it?

Cal is amazing. My advisor, John Bishop, is the author of *Joyce's Book of the Dark*, and he is considered one of the world's leading Joyce scholars, with a focus on *Finnegan's Wake*. He teaches Literary Theory and uses *Ulysses* as his textbook. Like most English majors, I've only read *Portrait of an Artist as a Young Man*. Joyce has this stream-of-consciousness thing going on, and he takes 10 years to destroy the English novel and recreate it in his own imaginings in *Ulysses*. And, being the masochist that I am, I decide to write my thesis on *Ulysses*. As I take this journey of one day in Dublin, which takes me four months, I contemplate an argument that Joyce is actually a realist, as he obviously lost his mind in the writing, thereby making me feel like I am losing *my* mind in the reading. As a mindful escape from my madness, I take poetry workshops with Robert Pinsky and Gary Soto. Gary reads my poems and tells me I need to start all over again. Self-reflection is a good thing for a writer.

WHAT DOES A POET LOOK LIKE?

Does she choreograph her poems
dancing through them with curly brown hair
tossing it back and forth in 3–3 time
looking for all the Earnest Young Men
rapidly grabbing them with guilt until they
Crack!

Or does she kiss New York hello
making angels in the brown snow of Queens.
Does her heart race underneath
like the subways?
Does she cook Alphabet poems
Does she fall like a leaf or
Explode like gunpowder!?
Does she change like the seasons
does she look like a poem?

Or does he have a beer-dripped beard?
Is he armed with a Heineken in constant motion,
up to the lips and down, up to the lips and down.
Does he give advice to middle-class clones
going to Mexico?
Does he drink as much on the weekends
playing softball
standing in right field
standing in the Upstart Crow
up to the lips and down, up to the lips and down.

Or does he stare at his poems
rolling dice along the pages?
Does he quiver like a Toyota on his way to Vegas?
Does he live in his car in the parking lot.
Is he buzzed on Morning Glory Seeds?
Does he eat peyote buds for breakfast
in a bowl with milk
snap, crackle, popping his mind.

Or is she a Mad Dog Black Lady
who walks you along the ghetto streets
leaving you breathless.
Is she passive aggressive
except when caught in mid-fuck.
Is she a big black nappy-haired vagina
Reading through her labia minora majora
with soouul and rhythmmm.
Is she a woman who wants to be loved
and known in the loving?

Or does she stand Under The Ladder
to Heaven
struggling to see through the Keyoto clouds
painfully reliving her abortion
compulsively pawing at her face.
Does she make you cry?

Or is he a big burly, bearded gray crotch
who's the leader of a pack of geriatric
patients in wheelchairs?
Or does he shuffle off to own up
to his own bullshit in Buffalo.
Does he slope towards the Equatorial Belt
looking like an Olympic Lifter?

Or does she have almond eyes?
Can you see the desert dust
falling from her lips as she reads?

Or does he wear a red beard
standing close by to all
ogling young poets with scrambled brains
journeying as a young child across the land
trying to hear the music?

What does a poet look like?
I certainly don't look like a poet
to the average guy.
For the poet traveled outside of himself.

That, any body can do
even the shit-throwing gorilla
in the San Diego Zoo
could be a poet.

I end up finding something interesting to say about the influence of Giordano Bruno on Joyce's overall structural writing. Most people look at the parallels with *The Odyssey*. I didn't want to do that. Only Joyce could've found inspiration in the writings of this turn-of-the-century Italian philosopher/priest who was burned to death by the church as a heretic on February 17, 1600. I graduate on May 20, 1988.

"Do not conform to the pattern of this world, but be transformed by the renewing of your mind. " Romans 12:2 (NIV)

10

Brave Heart

WE BUY OUR FIRST home that summer of '88. The house at 3302 Lowell Avenue in Richmond is a small, two-bedroom, one-bathroom ranch of approximately 950 square feet. It sits on a 50x100-foot lot with a single-car detached garage, a fenced-in back yard with a patio, and a lemon tree right outside the kitchen window. It's about 30 feet from the street, and there is a paved sidewalk. The neighborhood is usually quiet and well-kept but only a mile from 23rd Street—where death lives around the corner. Lowell is off of San Pablo Avenue, once one of the longest streets in the East Bay, running from Oakland to Pinole. San Pablo runs adjacent to I-80 so it's a quick exit and turn onto our block. There's only one stop sign, so bad guys frequently take Lowell down to 23rd after hopping off the freeway. We occasionally hear gunshots, and one night there is an explosion across the street. Our neighbor's son was selling crack and one of his dissatisfied customers, or possibly his supplier, decided to blow up the mailbox to send a loud message.

Paula is brave, but at times her righteous anger clouds her judgment and she places us in danger. We're leaving the house to go out to dinner one night, and we're about to get in our red Honda CRX, which is parked at the curb. A carload of bad guys come racing down the street and Paula yells out, "Slow down!" We get in the car; I'm in the driver's seat, and I watch through the rearview mirror as the driver turns the lights off, turns around and starts heading our way. My heart is now racing. The car pulls right up alongside us and stops with the windows rolled down. There are four young Hispanic men staring me down. They look surprised to see me. I'm dark and wearing my black leather jacket so they didn't see me when they drove by. They certainly saw Paula's long blonde hair. They don't say anything and after several long seconds they drive off. I just look at Paula; I don't say anything, and after several long seconds we drive off. This is not the last time we face danger at 3302 Lowell.

Another night we're walking to our car after leaving Tolman Hall. Parking is hard to find so our vehicle is a couple of blocks away in a residential area of mostly students. It's dark, not enough street-lights, and it's hard to see what's happening as we walk up on two young black men kicking a white man who's down on the ground next to his brown paper bag that was filled with groceries. We hear the thud of feet and the grunts of pain before we see what's going on. The robbers have already gotten what they wanted and were just releasing their anger upon this privileged grad student. They see us approaching, jump in their black Camaro and burn rubber in their flight from the scene. But before they are gone, Paula yells something, and I hear the tires squeal as the driver slams on the brakes. My heart is racing again but slows down after they decide to drive away. I say nothing to Paula and we both start helping the victim. We get him up and see that he is missing some teeth from having his face kicked in. We find four teeth on the sidewalk. He is a bloody mess, and we ask him if he wants us to call the police or take him to the hospital. He declines our offer and we help collect his groceries. He thanks us and walks away. As we're driving home, we think the guy was probably in shock and we should've done more. *We* were in shock.

We're totally clean and sober now, quitting weed after we bought our home. Paula's doing well in her program and in April '89, I get promoted to a supervisor position at the Juvenile Hall. The Diablo Unit, named after Mt. Diablo, which is visible to the east, houses boys ages 15 to 18. There are 100 beds, but we're usually overcrowded, with a daily population of around 120. It's a very hard place to be for the residents and the staff. Most of the kids are detained on pending cases waiting to go to court, but there are always kids—mostly convicted murderers—waiting for a bed to open up in the CYA, which is also overcrowded.

The promotion is a big deal for me. I competed through a written exam and interviewed to earn the number-one spot on a promotional list of 50 employees within the department. During my first meeting with the Chief and Deputy Chief, I'm told, in so many words, that this is the first step up the ladder to an upper-administrative position. I'm feeling pretty good about myself right now. I get home and can't wait to tell Paula the great news. When we finally sit down, I tell her the full story. She gives me a big smile and tells me how proud she is of me. We keep talking about my career, the retirement package, and where we want to live when we buy our second home, perhaps in the Berkeley Hills with a view of San Francisco. And as we talk, things start slowing down for me, and I begin to pick up on Paula's body language. Her smile slowly recedes and she's rubbing her hands together, which she does when she's nervous, and suddenly I see it in her eyes.

It's like nothing I've seen before; it's like God just gave me supernatural vision, because I see the light fading like a dimmer switch being turned down. And I know I can't do it; it's not part of the plan. I love California. It is the place where I have become a man, explored my ethnicity, reached a higher level of learning and love. I love the beaches in Southern California, the San Francisco Bay, the history, the ancient Redwoods. I see our lives in California, having a family, raising our kids. But I also see the light fading in her eyes. She misses her family. Every holiday, we go back East to be with family. I don't yet know how important family will be to me, but I know we have to eventually go back, and I tell her so.

My promotion to supervisor was sort of a set up. The qualifications for a group counselor present a low bar: high school diploma, some college, and no felony convictions. There is always plenty of overtime because of the abuse of sick leave. I know counselors who are making $90,000 a year, yet have only 30 college credits. People have mortgages, family ties and responsibilities, and sometimes folks get stuck. They can't afford to leave and have nowhere else to go. They become abusive burnouts, and I was promoted to clean house, to do what should've been done years ago.

I stay four months on the Diablo Unit, then get hired as a deputy probation officer . . . the job I really want, what God has been preparing me for. This is also achieved through a promotional list. Contra Costa County has some very specific promotion policies, which, I would later find out, resulted from some racial discrimination suits. My interview, again with the Chief and Deputy Chief Probation Officer, was interesting. The Deputy Chief, Carl Hopkins, is a paunchy, dark-skinned Black man in his mid-60s with a reputation for confrontation. At one point he looks at me and says, "I see you have an arrest for assault. What'd you do, beat somebody up?" Now I'm thinking, *that is essentially the definition, sir*, but reply, "I'd say it was a fair fight by way of mutual consent, and I got the better of my opponent." I knew how that sounded, my habitual New York sarcasm and arrogance, and I quickly rebounded with a fuller explanation of the circumstances at that time in my life, which led to the event.

I am assigned to the Adult Probation Office in Antioch, which is 30 miles from Richmond up State Route 4, which runs east parallel to the Sacramento River. Pittsburg, a once-thriving steel mill town—thus named after Pittsburgh, Pennsylvania—is just west of Antioch and very similar to Richmond since the steel industry has been gone for many years, and Pittsburg is another underserved minority community. I love the job, and they assign me a lot of younger probationers. I also get a few Spanish-speaking clients which gives me an opportunity to *praticar mi Espanol*. Half of my cases are for drunk driving, and I develop some competence in going over the standard and special conditions of probation in Spanish. This is done at the initial office visit, and one day I experience a strange response from a young man on probation for his second DUI.

Our appointment is scheduled for the afternoon, right after I return from Willie's Gym around the corner. By this time, I'm weighing 225 pounds and have 17-inch biceps at rest. I like to wear snug-fitting polo shirts to show off my guns. I'm very impressive. I'm meeting with my guy and still sweating from the gym. We're making it through the interview fairly well and I'm feeling quite confident in my Spanish until I tell him, "*Page con su muerta*," thinking I'm telling him he has to pay his fine. He seems confused and uncertain how to respond. By now I'm really hot, and the sweat is dripping into my right eye, irritating my contact lens, causing my eye to twitch. I think maybe he didn't hear me, so I lean in closer, sweating, eye twitching, biceps bulging and say again, only this time louder, "*Page con su muerta!*" Now the guy looks like he's about to jump out of his skin. He's nervous and looking around like he's thinking about running. I can see there's a big problem, and I say "*Uno momento por favor*" and call my bilingual supervisor, Simon Vasquez, for some help. He comes down and starts talking to the guy, who immediately relaxes, and the two of them look at me and start laughing. *Una Multa.* Simon says, "Ray, a fine is *una multa*. You were telling the guy that he has to pay with his death! He was terrified!"

Everything works out, and I learn a good lesson in Spanish. Simon and I hang out in my cubicle after the guy leaves, and we talk for a while. I can tell that he really wants to tell me something, and he eventually just brings it up because it's been bothering him. I knew that the second person on the supervisor list was Jerry Telez, a White guy who is well known for his competence and collegiality. He had worked as an adult probation officer for 15 years. The hiring committee first selected Jerry Telez for the job. The administration advised the committee that according to department practice (not policy), an individual in "a protected class" could not be passed over for promotion. They were instructed to change their forms and indicate that I was their selection. Simon then told me that this practice started after Carl Hopkins won a racial discrimination suit and was thereafter promoted.

I'm enraged. I'm not an expert but understand that affirmative action was to provide minorities with an equal opportunity, not an unfair advantage; the pursuit of diversity in the workplace should not be about quotas or fear of litigation, even though racial discrimination is real.

"Moreover, I saw under the sun that in the place of justice, even there was wickedness, and in the place of righteousness, even there was wickedness."
Ecclesiastes 3: 16,17 (ESV)

11

The Earth Quakes

ON OCTOBER 10, 1989, a 6.9 earthquake strikes the San Francisco Bay Area. It's 5:04 p.m., and I'm still at the probation office in Antioch, hanging out with a coworker, Jerry Homer, before heading home. I'm standing in his cubicle when things start shaking. I've been through at least a dozen earthquakes since living in California, and they've all been like a fun roller coaster ride for me. This one feels different. I feel a little nauseous and have a hard time moving because my equilibrium is off. And it goes on for a long time, longer than any quake I've experienced. It's exciting! On my way out I say to Jerry, "Man, that was a big one!" I get into my pickup truck and start driving. I'm looking forward to listening to the World Series between the Oakland Athletics and San Francisco Giants during the drive home.

I'm thinking about how different baseball fans are in the Bay Area. I've seen hundreds of people walking around with reversible caps that have the A's logo on one side and the Giants logo on the other. You would never see that in a subway series between the Yankees and the Mets. My cousin, Tom Lopez, and his wife, Pam, are at the game at Candlestick Park. Tom's a big Yankees fan. He and Pam are sitting in the nosebleed bleacher seats near the top of Candlestick. The stadium is packed. Fans are already stomping their feet in anticipation. Tom is a former Miami Beach narcotics detective and has a sharpened sense of his surroundings. He knows something major just happened and looks around to see that the wall behind him has a crack in it—wide enough to see into the parking lot—that wasn't there when they sat down! Tom and Pam are some of the first people to leave the stadium. Their drive home to Suisun City usually takes them 45 minutes. It takes them *six hours*.

When I turn on the radio, I immediately start listening to the broadcast about the earthquake and the scattered reports of the destruction it has caused. I hear about the collapse of the Cypress Freeway in Oakland and also a section of the Bay Bridge. I'm not sure where Paula is today. I know she was at Skyline High School in Oakland yesterday, and she's also been working in the Alameda schools, which takes her over the Cypress—usually a parking lot at this time of the day. I also hear a story about fires breaking out in Berkeley. My mind races with the morbid possibilities.

When I get home, my neighbor runs up to my truck with a large wrench in his hand and says that we have to turn the gas off on all the houses. I tell him okay, and he runs around the side of my house to take care of it. He's very handy, and it's a good thing because my primary skill is to pick up heavy things and put them down. When I walk through the front door it looks like a tornado has come through the house. Everything that was hanging on the walls is now on the floor, and all the dressers have tipped over because the drawers rolled out during the shaking. There's no cable or phone service and no way to contact Paula. I can't remember her schedule for the day, and there's no way for me to get in touch with her. Paula was in class on the fifth floor of the five-story Tollman Hall when the earthquake struck. The building was evacuated and classes were cancelled. She gets home at 6:30 p.m.

The cable is back up later that night, and phone services are restored by the next day. We've been watching the news. There are still over 60 vehicles trapped in the collapsed section of I-880, the Cypress Freeway. Paula was driving on it the day before and would've been in that section sitting in traffic at around the time of the quake. Fortunately, the Bay Bridge Series saves hundreds of lives, as the estimated 200 drivers that would've been sitting in traffic were either home, at a bar, or at the stadium getting ready to watch the game. We sit in horror watching the video of that disoriented driver in the little red car who drove off the end of the collapsed section of the Bay Bridge. Most of our family and friends know that we drive a little red Honda CRX, and we get a number of calls to make sure it wasn't us who drove off the bridge.

Sixty-three people die under the Cypress Freeway, 3,800 are injured, and six billion in property damage is caused by the San Francisco Bay Area Earthquake. Now I don't enjoy earthquakes as much. There's a major shift in attitude about living in the Bay Area after the quake, and many people move away. There's also a seismic shift about to come into our lives.

Like Orange County, Contra Costa County Probation has a mandatory 40-hour per year training requirement, but it is all either done or arranged by the department. One day I'm in a session with a few officers from Federal Probation. I have never heard of them but okay, there's a federal probation system. It makes sense. They put on a presentation about the Federal Sentencing Guidelines. I'm looking at criminal history categories and offense severity levels and a sentencing chart with 252 possible sentencing ranges. "*Oh the humanity!*" A few months later Simon tells me about a job opening and convinces me to apply.

The Chief's assistant calls, and we set up an appointment for my interview. On the designated day, I put on my best suit and go to the most important interview of my life. I ride the BART into downtown San Francisco and walk into the U.S. Courthouse wearing my gray-striped jacket, pleated gray slacks that almost match, light-gray Italian shoes, a white shirt, and my red paisley tie . . . the only tie I own. I look like a drug dealer on Miami Vice. Nobody looks like me. They're all wearing navy-blue blazers, black or gray slacks, a white shirt and solid color ties, but the darker shades like brown and black and blue. I'm interviewed in the conference room by Chief Probation Officer Loren Buddres, Deputy Chief Frank Vasquez, and a few of the supervisors. After it's over, I feel really good about it; I feel those good, good, good, good vibrations.

A week later I get called in for a second interview. This time I arrive wearing my brand-new navy-blue blazer, dark gray slacks, plain black shoes, white shirt, and solid red tie. The interview is great, more like a conversation. Toward the end, this grouchy

HARD LOVE

supervisor playing bad cop says to me, "You know we have a dress code around here; I noticed what you wore at the first interview. Do you think you'll have any difficulty complying with our code?" to which I reply, "How do you like me now?" as I straighten my tie. New Yorkers are so sarcastic, but I know this guy is originally from Brooklyn and will appreciate it. I start my career as a federal probation officer in Oakland on October 8, 1990.

Federal is the major leagues of the probation/parole world. We spend around $2000 to get me a professional wardrobe. 'Crime and punishment' has to be shared with the state and local authorities, but there are routine cases for the Feds like bank robbery of a federally insured bank, bank fraud, securities fraud, and tax offenses. Anything that affects interstate compacts could be a federal case: narcotics, firearms, explosives, child pornography offenses—any crime that involves the use of a phone and/or the U.S. Mail. Joint federal and state task force work is the way to go so that everyone gets their piece of the pie. But we get the big cases, and defendants are facing real time. The 1984 Sentencing Reform Act eliminates parole and establishes federal sentencing guidelines to reduce disparity around the country and bring honesty to sentencing. But in 1985, Congress enacts the Anti-Drug Abuse Act, which establishes mandatory minimum terms of imprisonment triggered by the quantities of heroin, crack, and powder cocaine. This trumps the Guidelines and reminds me of my political science course at Saddleback and my textbook, *The Perverted Priorities of American Government.* Congress gives birth to a kind of bastard child between itself and the Judicial Branch when it creates the Sentencing Commission to promulgate guidelines, but then creates mandatory minimums the next year. The inmates who behave well will serve 87% of their sentence and then start serving an additional term of supervised release.

During my first week in the Oakland office, as part of my training, I'm assigned to spend the day with a senior officer. I get placed with Special Offender Specialist Joe Lopez, no relation. He's a doubly special guy. The highlight of my day is meeting Sonny Barger, a founding member of the Oakland Chapter of the Hells Angels. He comes in for his office visit with his agent to seek permission to leave the state to work as a consultant on a movie. I know I'm going to love this job.

All the writing I've done in school serves me well for such a time as this. I am assigned to the presentence unit. I do presentence investigations-PSIs. I interview the defendant, family members, victims, prosecutors, agents, probation officers, parole officers, employers, teachers, coaches, pastors, priests . . . to whosoever the case leads me. And I do the paper chase, going after vital records—educational, vocational, medical, treatment—and so it goes. At the conclusion of my investigation, I write a presentence report which includes a narrative of the offense, an analysis of the Sentencing Guidelines and criminal history, personal and family history, my evaluation of the case, and a sentencing recommendation. Thereafter, I go into chambers to meet with the judge and talk about the case. There is clearly a professional writing style that sets certain parameters. But this is the Bay Area, and there is a spirit of acceptance and open-mindedness that influences everything. So I get to push the envelope a little. In one evaluation on a sophisticated fraudster who had numerous aliases, shell corporations, and off-shore accounts, there was nothing more apt to say in my summary but, "Oh what a tangled web we weave, when first we practice to deceive." — *Macbeth*

"Then a great and powerful wind tore the mountains apart and shattered rocks before the Lord, but the Lord was not in the wind. After the wind there was an earthquake, but the Lord was not in the earthquake. After the earthquake came a fire. And after the fire came a gentle whisper." 1 Kings 19: 11,12 (NIV)

12

Tebben from Heaven

PAULA IS PREGNANT! THE timing couldn't have been more perfect. Her due date was the same date as the last day of her internship in the Alameda Public Schools. A control freak's dream. We start taking a Lamaze class at Alta Bates Hospital in Berkeley, where we meet Keith Jones and Alison Kirby Jones. Alison received her PhD in Business from Stanford and was teaching at Cal. I run into Keith one day in the elevator of the federal building in San Francisco where he just finished videotaping a deposition. He runs his own small production company and is an aspiring screenplay writer. Through the birth of our children we become close friends.

The time of Paula's pregnancy is a blur to me but for Valentine's Day in February 1991. We're meeting for lunch at a restaurant in Jack London Square. I can walk there from my office on Broadway in Downtown Oakland, and Paula is coming from Alameda. I pick up a dozen roses on the way there and spend a long time selecting a card, almost fifteen minutes. I don't write her a poem, but meditate deeply on the words I write in her card. We sit down in one of our favorite restaurants. She is so beautiful. It is the beginning of her second trimester. She's been wearing her hair short for a while now. Her Beatles cut makes her look like a young squire in King Arthur's Court.

I can see something's wrong. She tells me she doesn't like flowers, and that stopping to pick up a card on the way to lunch doesn't show much thought. I want to tell her that I did give it a lot of thought. I didn't know she didn't like flowers, and I intentionally waited until today to pick out a card to be so inspired by the spontaneity of our love. But I think it not wise to say so at the time. Three months and 27 hours of labor later, Paula goes into surgery for an emergency C-section. They let me in the room and I'm sitting beside her, our faces close together. There is a curtain hiding her midsection. This is the procedure developed as a result of the history of fainting fathers. Paula has suffered long and hard but isn't feeling any pain when they start to pull our child from her womb. I see huge shoulders, a full head of black hair and shout, "It's a boy! It's a boy!" The doctor looks at me and says, "Mr. Lopez, you might want to wait until the whole baby is out." And in the next moment I see and shout, "It's a girl! It's a girl!"

Like most men, I wanted a boy, but the moment I meet Tebben Gill Lopez on June 27, 1991, I cannot conceive of a greater gift from God. Paula and Tebben stay at the hospital overnight, and the next day I find Keith and Alison in the room next door. Alison's water has broken, and she is beginning to dilate. All three members of our new family visit with them on and off through the day. During one visit, Tebben gives out a healthy cry, and the nurse comes running in with a look of disbelief on her face, thinking that Alison popped out her baby on her own. Forrest is born the next day.

When Tebben is a few months old, Paula begins taking her to Judson Memorial Baptist Church, a couple of blocks down the street. When she comes home, I just watch and listen to her talk about the service and the people. Occasionally I ask questions, but I'm not so sure it's the place for me to go. I am sure that Paula is happy—and that makes me happy. She eventually asks if it would be okay to invite the pastor over for a visit and I say sure. Pastor David Yetter comes by one day and we hang out and talk. He and his wife, Sandy, are around our age and have four kids, including their baby boy, Jonathan, who's a year older than Tebb. We hit it off. He's passionate about having a personal relationship with God and growing closer to him through gathering in worship and prayer and living and learning through scripture.

We start attending Judson as a family, join the choir, and sometimes sing special music and duets. It's a diverse congregation representative of the community: White, Black, Hispanic, Asian, multigenerational families. And it is a family. We meet for Bible study and choir practice during the week and have a meal together in the church basement on Sundays after services. We spend a lot of time with the Yetters, and Sandy starts babysitting for Tebb. David's a good preacher in the Baptist tradition, with a focus on the Gospel and saving the lost, which is close to my heart. My identity as an evangelist is affirmed and strengthened. I feel at peace, which is good because there's a lot of unrest in the neighborhood.

Home burglaries are occurring, and people are getting tense. One Sunday morning at around 7 a.m., I hear scratching outside the window at the head of our bed. I pull the curtain back and see a face disappear. I jump up, grab my Louisville Slugger and start running around the block to see if I can find the guy. It's very quiet. Nobody saw anything. Paula also encounters a peeper through the bathroom window while naked in the shower. Next Sunday night, Jim Lee, a new officer I am mentoring, comes over for dinner and to join us for Sunday night service. When we get back to the house, I see that someone has broken in. The glass slats from the jalousie window in the kitchen have been removed. I look in our bedroom and see our VCR lying on the bed near an open window, which means they were in the house when we got home! Again I grab my bat, and Jim and I run around the neighborhood. Thank God we don't find any suspicious characters because I don't know what could've happened. Our total loss is around $7000—$4000 of it from a family heirloom given to me by my mother after her Padrino passed away. It's a 22-karat-gold medallion from Spain. It's so heavy that I have to shorten the chain because I'm getting bruises on my sternum. Fortunately, we have a photo of the piece and insurance covers it.

But there are still bad guys racing down the street. One Saturday afternoon I'm relaxing on the couch, reading *Childhood's End* by Arthur C, Clark, when a car speeds by and Paula screams, "Slow down!" at the top of her lungs. I figure they hear her because the driver slams on his brakes so hard the front left hubcap comes flying off. Paula is standing behind the front screen door with Tebben in her arms! My hearts starts racing again, and I realize how exposed we are with the door wide open. I close the inner door and essentially hide my family in our home, praying whoever they are won't come back and figure out what house the scream came from. I feel like a coward, but I know I'm being smart. This time I have a few instructive words for Paula after they drive away.

Fear gnaws at your heart. On April 29, 1992, a jury in the Los Angeles suburb of Simi Valley acquits the four White officers charged with excessive force in arresting Rodney King, a young black man on parole, a year earlier. The verdicts ignite the L.A. Riots. After they are read, we watch a news reporter on TV standing on a street corner saying, "So far it's quiet here in L.A. Nothing's happening." He might as well have said, "Where are you people? Why isn't anybody doing anything?!" Fear gnaws at your heart. We watch on live TV as Reginald Denny, a White truck driver, is dragged from his truck on the corner of Florence and Normandie streets and savagely beaten by several rioters. One young Black man skips into the picture, carrying a large brick in his hand, and joyfully skips off after smashing the brick down on Denny's head. Another walks up with what appears to be a sawed-off shotgun, but the gun jams when he tries to blow Denny's head off. The city is on fire with rampant looting and destruction. Innocent people are pulled from their cars and beaten. Korean store owners stand guard with firearms trying to protect their property. Fear gnaws at your heart.

The next day I take Tebben for a walk down the block in the stroller. I see a group of Black teenagers walking in our direction. I cross the street. Fear gnaws at your heart. When I go to work the following Monday, while crossing Broadway to enter the office, I see a couple of young Black men in a white Cadillac turn the corner. The car accelerates rapidly in my direction, and I have to jump to the curb to avoid being struck. Fear gnaws at your heart, but I know ". . . the Spirit God gave us does not make us timid, but gives us power, love and self-discipline." 2 Timothy 1:7

But life goes on, as always, and now it's the four of us at 3302 Lowell Avenue—Paula, Tebben, me, and "Mama's Stupid Dissertation." I never should've called it that in front of Tebben. Her first words are "bye bye!" inspired by hearing 'bye bye' from her mama every day before leaving for school. It's hard being apart from Paula. But God calls me and Tebben to the Oakland Zoo, where we visit the pink flamingos, the peacocks, and our favorite, Mr. Bengal Tiger, at least three times a week. They also have a carousel and cotton candy. Tebben and I form a solid bond that is strong and alive today.

Our family portrait

"For I know the plans I have for you," declares the LORD, "plans to prosper you and not to harm you, plans to give you hope and a future." Jeremiah 29:11 (NIV)

13

Baptism

THERE'S A LARGE BAPTISMAL behind the alter at Judson, essentially a huge bathtub. This figures. It's a Baptist church. People get baptized. I was baptized as an infant at Christ the King in Commack, but it's of no importance to me. I have come to jokingly describe myself as a recovering Catholic. We know the Gospel. We know the story of John the Baptist, who baptized Jesus, which was a big deal to God as he opened up Heaven and sent down the Holy Spirit to fill his son. Pastor Yetter teaches that baptism isn't essential to know Christ, but it is a public declaration of faith that God will bless. Paula has never been publicly baptized and is excited about doing it. I decide to do it with her, with no great expectations.

There is a baptismal service that the entire church attends. Gloria has been staying with us for a while to help with Tebben while Paula finishes her dissertation and reads Paula's testimony before the baptism, which given the fact that she is an nonbeliever, is a miracle. Paula goes in the water first. David stands behind her and supports her as she leans back—submerged—and emerges in Glory. She steps down into my arms, and I have never seen such tears of joy. I have never seen her so happy. She shudders as wave after wave of the Holy Spirit flows through her until she gently rests on my shoulder and is wrapped in a towel by other church members. Now it's my turn. I feel good. I feel strong in the Lord. I've been memorizing scripture and have been bold in my faith in the community. I led my coworker, Jim Lee, to accept Christ, and everyone who knows me knows I'm a Christian. I'm just going to get a little wet, that's all.

I go in the water and it feels like I'm under a long time, like time is suspended. I feel the cold, and although my vision is blurred, I see two dark shadows, like clouds in the water. My demons have been chasing me to the finish. (Years later at a prophetic service in Massachusetts, I received a word of knowledge from a prophet who knew I had been in jail and told me that two large angels, with armor and swords, have been fighting for my soul.) But I come up from the water into an actual beam of sunlight that is shining through a window. And I have victory that day, and I pray that I will resist temptation every day and that my demons will remain permanent fugitives from my life.

"Are not all the angels ministering spirits sent out [by God] to serve (accompany, protect) those who will inherit salvation? [Of course they are!]
Hebrews 1:14 (AMP)

14

Take Me Home

PAULA'S DISSERTATION FOCUSES ON resilience in middle school students at risk of dropping out. Her time working at Richmond High School provides her an "in" to obtain ample subjects for her doctoral project. She is the Director of the Richmond Human Relations Academy, under the auspices of the Human Relations Department. She and her colleagues work with select fifth- and sixth-graders across the district who are leaders among their peers, but just leading in the wrong direction. The Department establishes a data-driven student-centric crisis intervention team and gang intervention outreach led by former gang members.

Paula's review committee is prestigious, starting with Nadine Lambert, the director of Paula's program and a giant in the field of School Psychology. She is literally a giant of a woman. My favorite Nadine story is when she is in an airport flying standby to a conference with one of her graduate students, who is recovering from a sprained ankle. They hear a last-minute scheduling change over the loudspeaker on their flight, and in order to make it on time, Nadine lifts her 100-pound student and hurries with the student under her arm, like a football, to the gate!

Opportunity forces me to consider withdrawing my only condition on moving back east, that being the filing of one's dissertation. Paula starts applying early for a tenure-track position to schools in the tri-state area and is one of two final candidates being considered for a position at St. John's University in Queens. In preparation for this possibility, I secure a transfer to the Presentence Investigation Unit in Brooklyn. Paula flies out for the interview, and when she gets back, upon reflection, she is feeling good about the visit and excited about becoming part of the School Psychology Department at St. John's. I'm *not* feeling good, and I'm *not* excited about relocating back east and working in Brooklyn. Like she did when I was offered the ladder to success in Contra Costa County, I am trying to say the right things and have a supportive attitude as we wait to hear from the hiring committee, making sure she sees no dimming light in my eyes. And when the rejection comes, I offer her comfort and say the right things before I go into the back yard and praise the Lord!

A new round of academic position announcements come out the following year and Paula is scheduled for interviews at The University of Connecticut and Fairfield University in Fairfield, Connecticut. I have been in contact with Maria Rodriguez McBride, Chief Probation Officer in the District of Connecticut, about a possible transfer. To transfer to Brooklyn, I had to submit five samples of presentence reports I prepared and fill out another federal application form. In contrast, Maria and I are just talking. We travel as a family this time, and I meet with Maria and her management staff during our stay. She promises me a job when one becomes available.

In stark contrast to her UCONN interview experience, during her interview at Fairfield, Paula is falling in love with the place. When she's left alone to prepare for her teaching demonstration, she prays to God, "Lord, I really like these people and if you want me to come here, I would really like to come here." Immediately after her prayer, the search committee chair pops her head in the office and says, "I just spoke to the Dean, and his first choice is the search committee's first choice—you." When she pops out again Paula says, "Thank you, Jesus!"

And so it goes. Paula accepts the job at Fairfield, and a position opens up for me in the Bridgeport Federal Probation Office. We quickly sell our home for $127,000—earning $20,000 in equity—adding to the moving stipend Fairfield offers, which we use for moving expenses, including having our three cars towed back along with our furniture. We spend the last few months renting the upstairs section of our realtor's home with a view of the Bay. The lights of San Francisco at night somewhat softens my growing sorrow over our pending departure.

Pressure at Cal also pushes Paula, when one of her readers, Dr. Rona Weinstein, is not willing to sign off on her dissertation and raises a fundamental issue about Paula's research, saying, "Your analysis does not answer the interesting question you originally asked." (In the end, Rona was right, and Paula's work becomes much more important as a result). The next year, Rona is named UC Berkeley's Distinguished Professor of the Year and invites Paula to write a letter for her and attend the ceremony. We both have starting dates in September, and we book our flight with Tower Airlines, direct from LAX to JFK. We get to spend a week with Denise and Mark and their daughters in San Juan Capistrano before we go. It's relaxing, but that all changes when we make it to LAX on August 1, 1994, for a red-eye arriving at JFK the next day.

Tebben is now three years old and an experienced flyer, but nothing in her experience, or ours for that matter, has prepared her for this. When we get to the gate an hour early, a few minutes before the flight, we find out that there is a mechanical problem with the plane, which is causing an indefinite delay. And so we stay in the gate area along with the other passengers from our fully booked flight, made up of New Yorkers and Israelis returning to Tel Aviv. As the hours tick by, we receive additional information: a part has to be replaced (they're careful not to tell us what kind of part), and they have to send out for it!

And so we wait, but things get difficult when we are told that the crew has timed out and they have to assemble a new crew! Again, we are part of a gathering of 150 New Yorkers and Israelis, embattled generational suffering mixed with unconscious ethnocentrism and a seasoning of sarcasm. There are no shops or restaurants in the Tower Air terminal. Nothing. We have walked back and forth with Tebben in the stroller around the outside of this massive airport; it's been almost 10 hours and we are finally lining up to board the plane! But the line isn't moving. The shit almost hits the proverbial fan, when I approach the attendant at the door to the plane for an explanation and she says, "I'm sorry, sir, but they are cleaning the plane now which will take a few more minutes." I respond with "What? The jet has been in the terminal for twelve hours, and you're telling me you are just now cleaning the plane!" I almost blow it in my small moment of anxious expression. A wave of tension spreads through that line of passengers like falling dominoes, and I feel the edge of a mob about to crash through.

We finally board and settle in our seats in front of the flight attendants' station, which provides extra legroom and space for Tebb to crawl around. The plane takes off; I feel a part of me dying, and I cry. I've grown into manhood in California and left childish things behind. I married Paula, stopped drinking and drugging, was baptized in the Holy Spirit, found a church, found a career, earned a graduate degree, bought a home, and was there to see Tebben enter the world. Halfway through the flight, Tebb is tired and cold, so I ask a flight attendant for a blanket so she can take a nap on the floor at our feet. I'm not surprised when she tells me there are no more blankets available. But I am surprised by the act of kindness shown by the oversized lady sitting across the aisle. She loans us a pair of her shorts—which make a perfect blanket—and Tebb sleeps away until she is awoken by the pain in her ears popping to the pressure of our descent.

It's been a long, hard journey back east, and I know I cannot go forward in my own strength. No.

But I also know I won't have to.

"I can do all things through Christ who strengthens me."
Philippians 4:13 (NKJV)

Made in the USA
Las Vegas, NV
25 October 2022

58152482R00056